Grace at the Table

Ending Hunger in God's World

by

David Beckmann
and
Arthur Simon

Paulist Press
New York/Mahwah, N.J.

To

Bread for the World
members

a gift of grace
to hungry people

Cover design by Cynthia Dunne

Cover illustration courtesy Bread for the World Institute

Book design by Saija Autrand, Faces Type & Design

Clip art from MasterClips

Library of Congress Cataloging-in-Publication Data

Beckmann, David M.
    Grace at the table: ending hunger in God's world / by David Beckmann and Arthur Simon.
      p. cm.
    Includes bibliographical references.
    ISBN 0–8091–3866–2 (alk. paper)
    1. Food supply—Government policy.   2. Agriculture and state.   3. Hunger.
I. Simon, Arthur R.   II. Title.
HD9000.5.B39   1999
338.1'9—dc21   99-13994
                                                      CIP

Published by Paulist Press
997 Macarthur Boulevard
Mahwah, New Jersey 07430

www.paulistpress.com

Printed and bound in the United States of America

Contents

Hunger
in
God's World

Chapter 1

A Place at the Table

A large family is seated at a dinner table. They bow their heads and together acknowledge that the food set before them and the life it sustains are gifts from God. They say grace.

After the prayer, a few children quickly scoop up most of the food. Others at the table go hungry. Gaunt looks on several faces indicate that this happens regularly. Grace at the table has been violated by an injustice that contradicts the goodness of the Giver, for truly to thank God is also to share the gift of food with everyone at the table.

Unfortunately, this imaginary scene is a snapshot of the human family today, because more than 800 million people in the developing countries still suffer chronic undernutrition. About 31 thousand children under age five die each day in developing countries, half from hunger-related causes.

In the United States 34 million people live in families that are food insecure, and the number of people who sometimes go hungry in the United States has probably increased over the last 25 years.[1]

Yet widespread hunger is no longer necessary. Wars and tyrants will cause some people to go hungry, no matter what we do. But the resources, technology and knowledge needed to end the sort of routine, pervasive hunger the world now tolerates are readily available. Ending hunger, in this sense, is quite feasible worldwide. It's even more clear that most of the hunger in the United States could be eliminated, because other countries at the same level of average per capita income have done so.

A generation ago, scientists and government leaders realized that for the first time the world had the means to overcome hunger. At the World Food Conference in 1974 U.S. Secretary of State Henry A. Kissinger, citing political will as the critical factor in overcoming hunger, proposed and the conference resolved "that within a decade no child will go to bed hungry."[2] President

Gerald Ford then commissioned a National Academy of Sciences study, which confirmed that lack of political will more than anything else prevented the eradication of hunger. A few years later, President Jimmy Carter's commission on world hunger concluded that "if decisions and actions well within the capability of nations and people working together were implemented, it would be possible to eliminate the worst aspects of hunger and malnutrition by the year 2000."[3] But the United States did not, as both commissions urged, make this a major policy objective.

All of us stand on the threshold of a new millennium. Progress has been made. In the developing countries, the proportion of the population that is hungry has decreased over the last 25 years from one-third to one-fifth. And even though the population of those countries grew substantially, fewer people there are hungry now than in 1970.

God is giving us an opportunity to reduce human suffering dramatically. Hunger, though complex, can be overcome. The key is for each of us to help change the politics of hunger. That, in a nutshell, is the message of this book.

You may not like politics or think of yourself as a political person, but if you are concerned about hungry people, stick with us. We'll explain why government policies are an essential but neglected part of the solution to hunger. We'll show how you can use your power as a citizen to help end hunger. That's of critical importance. Peter Maurin, who helped Dorothy Day start the Catholic Worker movement, once said, "The world is full of people who either think but fail to act or who act but fail to think." We challenge you to think *and* act, because what you do, or fail to do, has an impact on people's lives.

You deserve to know who the authors are and the backgrounds that shape our thinking. One of us (Simon) worked for a decade as a pastor in the economically deprived Lower East Side of New York City. In 1972 he began searching for a way that concerned Christians could more effectively influence U.S. government policies that were having a big and often negative impact on hungry people in this country and abroad. He and a few others decided to launch Bread for the World, first locally and then, in 1974, nationwide. Simon became Bread for the World's founding president.

The other author (Beckmann) was called at his ordination

to be a "missionary economist." After serving in a church-sponsored development agency in Bangladesh, he worked for 15 years on antipoverty efforts in dozens of developing countries for the World Bank. His last assignment there was to lead the Bank's growing engagement with grass-roots organizations around the world. Since 1991 he has been president of Bread for the World.

Bread for the World is a Christian citizens' movement against hunger. Its purpose is to build U.S. political will for ending hunger. Its 44 thousand members urge—and often succeed in getting—Congress to adopt policies and pass specific laws that help reduce hunger. Bread for the World is a lively grass-roots movement, with volunteer leaders in communities and on campuses across the country.

The Bread for the World Institute, a partner organization, does research and education on hunger. The Institute networks with groups around the world on hunger issues, trains anti-hunger leaders and prepares educational materials such as this book.

Each year Bread for the World asks churches and other groups to take part in a nationwide Offering of Letters. Churches ask their members to learn about a specific hunger issue and then consider writing a letter to Congress. The annual Offering of Letters mobilizes as many as 100 thousand letters to Congress to get action on hunger legislation. Bread for the World's membership spans the spectrum of Catholics, evangelical and mainline Protestants and Orthodox Christians. It also includes people of other faiths and people who profess no particular faith but are drawn by the importance of its work.

Hunger cuts across religious lines and invites a response from all people of good will, but sometimes in this book we speak to a primarily Christian audience. Christians believe in a God of grace. *Grace* means "gift," first and foremost the gift of God's undeserved love for us in Jesus Christ, whose life, death and resurrection rescue us from sin and give us eternal life. In Christ, God reaches out in love to all people—to those who don't have enough to eat and to those who find it easy to ignore others in need. Because we are saved by grace for the purpose of giving our lives to works of love (Eph 2:8–10), God's grace can powerfully motivate us to help end hunger.

Christians not only have the motivation of God's great love

and purpose but are especially well positioned by virtue of affluence, influence and global distribution to take the lead in ending
hunger. If U.S. Christians expanded their assistance through
private agencies and played a stronger role in advocating policy
initiatives, they could quickly become the driving force toward
ending hunger everywhere. What a blessing and what a witness
that would be!

Given the fact that humankind has the means to end hunger, its persistence in God's world is a scandal. It is a scandal not
only in the sense of moral outrage, but also because it causes
despair and alienates people from God. This is an abundant
world. Yet, while much of the world (including most of us in the
United States) is feasting, part of the human family has no
secure place at the table.

It doesn't have to be that way.

Every time we say grace before a meal, we are reminded that
daily bread is indeed a gift to share. Every time Christians gather
to share the cup of blessing and break the bread of life together,
we remember the death and resurrection of Jesus—God's gift of
grace, which impels us to be grace-giving to others. We are all
inclined to neglect that purpose and go about other business. But
God forgives, again and again. God's mercy embraces us; God is
always eager for a response.

Each of us can take at least one step toward ending hunger
in God's world. The authors hope this book will help you take
that step, and that you will take it not as a burden, but as a celebration of grace.

Chapter 2

What God Intends

> Is not this the fast that I choose:
> to loose the bonds of injustice,
> to undo the thongs of the yoke,
> to let the oppressed go free,
> and to break every yoke?
>
> If you offer your food to the hungry
> and satisfy the needs of the afflicted,
> then your light shall rise in the darkness
> and your gloom be like the noonday.
> —*Isaiah 58:6, 10*[1]

The Bible leaves no room for doubt about God's intention for us. God embraces us in love and stirs us to seek justice for those who are oppressed.

What is God's intention, more specifically, regarding hunger?

Two main themes run through the Bible concerning hunger. The first is God's providence. The second is our responsibility to take care of the earth and one another. Both themes reflect the will of God that everyone be adequately fed.

These themes emerge in the very first pages of the Old Testament or Hebrew scriptures, when God places Adam and Eve in a lush garden with an abundance of food and tells them to replenish the earth and take care of it. The subsequent account of Cain murdering his brother Abel sends the clear message from God that we *are* our brother's and sister's keeper.

The theme of God's providence becomes part of the prophetic vision of a time when there will be no more hunger. Isaiah wrote, "On this mountain the Lord of hosts will make for all peoples a feast of rich food, a feast of well-aged wines, of rich food filled with marrow, of well-aged wines strained clear" (25:6). Although we look for the complete fulfillment of this promise in heaven, we also pray with Jesus, "Thy will be done on earth as it is in heaven."

Both themes—God's providence and our responsibility for one another—emerge dramatically in the exodus from Egypt. God's liberation of the Hebrew people from slavery echoes through the entire Old Testament, informing its faith and its ethical instruction. Consider the great silent *therefore* that precedes and applies to all Ten Commandments. "I am the Lord your God, who brought you out of the land of Egypt, out of the house of slavery; [therefore] you shall have no other gods before me" (Ex 20:2–3). God's love for the oppressed Israelites forms a basis both for our response to God and for the way we are to relate to one another. The exodus experience shaped the laws, informed the prophets and became deeply embedded in the worship of the Hebrew people.

How is this exodus experience connected to hunger?

Over and over the law instructs Israelites to remember the foreigner (i.e., the immigrant), the orphan and the widow—those most vulnerable to hunger and poverty—and ties this instruction to the exodus. Look at Deuteronomy:

> When you gather your crops and fail to bring in some of the grain that you have cut, do not go back for it; it is to be left for the foreigners, orphans and widows. . . . When you have gathered your grapes once, do not go back over the vines a second time; the grapes that are left are for the foreigners, orphans and widows. Never forget that you were slaves in Egypt; that is why I have given you this command.
>
> *(24:19–22 TEV)*

Other laws provided for sharing one-tenth of the harvest with immigrants, orphans and widows (Dt 14:28–29), for lending at no interest to those in need (Ex 22:25) and for the cancellation of debts every seventh year (Dt 15:1–2, 7–11). Every fiftieth year was to be a year of jubilee, during which property was to be returned to the family of the original owner. The intent of this law, which may never have been carried out, was to prevent the concentration of wealth and make sure that each family had the means to feed itself.

The prophets, too, insisted on justice for everyone. Amos, for example, denounced those who trampled on the needy and destroyed the poor in order to gain wealth. He railed against those who lived in luxury while the poor were being crushed.

The prophets' main judgments were leveled against idolatry and social injustice. The living God insists on personal morality and social justice, while idols offer fertility and prosperity without social responsibility.

The Psalms (the hymns of ancient Israel) invite us to celebrate God's justice.

> [God] always keeps his promises;
> he judges in favor of the oppressed
> and gives food to the hungry.   *(146:6–7 TEV)*

> Happy are those who are concerned for the poor;
> the Lord will help them when they are in trouble.
> *(41:1 TEV)*

The wisdom literature in the Old Testament expresses the same theme, as these texts from Proverbs indicate:

> If you refuse to listen to the cry of the poor,
> your own cry will not be heard.   *(21:13 TEV)*

> Speak out for those who cannot speak,
> for the rights of all the destitute.
> [D]efend the rights of the poor and needy.
> *(31:8–9)*

Concern for poor, hungry and vulnerable people is pervasive in the Hebrew scriptures. It flows directly from the revelation of God through the rescue of an enslaved people.

And in the New Testament?

The New Testament ethic builds on the Hebrew scriptures. Like them, it does not simply offer a platter of moral advice. Its teachings emerge from a divine act of salvation—the life, death and resurrection of Jesus Christ. Because "the lamb of God who takes away the sin of the world" conquered sin and death for us, we are forgiven, reconciled to God, born anew to be imitators of God, called to sacrificial love for others. Through the gift of eternal life, Jesus sets us free to make the doing of good our purpose in life (Eph 2:8–10).

The nature of the good we are to do is not left in doubt, for we have the example of Jesus himself. He had a special sense of mission to poor and oppressed people—evidence that, in him, the messianic promises were being fulfilled. At the outset of his ministry, Jesus stood up in the synagogue at Nazareth and read from the prophet Isaiah:

> The Spirit of the Lord is upon me,
> because he has anointed me to bring good news to the poor.
> He has sent me to proclaim release to the captives
> and recovery of sight to the blind,
> to let the oppressed go free,
> to proclaim the year of the Lord's favor.
>
> *(Lk 4:18–19)*

The gospels depict Jesus repeatedly reaching out to those at the bottom of the social pyramid—poor people, women, Samaritans, lepers, children, prostitutes and tax collectors. Jesus was also eager to accept people who were well-placed, but he made clear that all, regardless of social position, needed to repent. For this reason he invited the rich young lawyer to sell all of his possessions and give the proceeds to the poor.

"Blessed are you who are poor," said Jesus in Luke's version of the Sermon on the Mount, and he added, "But woe to you who are rich, for you have received your consolation" (6:20, 24). Jesus once said, "[I]t is easier for a camel to go through the eye of a needle than for someone who is rich to enter the kingdom of God" (Mk 10:25). The point is stark, intended to shock us—but how many sermons have you heard on it? We tend to duck, for in few aspects of life are we so prone to idolatry and self-deception as in matters concerning our own material advantage.

In his portrayal of the day of judgment, Jesus pictured people from all nations gathered before him. To the "sheep" he says, "Come you blessed of my Father, for I was hungry and you fed me. . . ." In their astonishment they ask, "When did we do that?" And he answers, "When you did it to the lowliest of my brothers [and sisters]." Conversely, to the "goats" he says, "Out of my sight, you who are condemned, for I was hungry and you did not feed me . . ." (Mt 25:31–46).[2]

Clearly, in both Old and New Testaments the intention of God that all people find a place at the table is combined with a responsibility on our part for those who are most vulnerable, those most often kept from the table. This intention flows from the heart of God, who reaches out in love to all of us—rich, poor and in-between.

We have obligations, but so do the poor.
Aren't people often poor and hungry because they are lazy, and others rich because they've worked hard?

Yes, poor people have obligations. The apostle Paul said, "Anyone unwilling to work should not eat" (2 Thes 3:10). But poor people have no monopoly on laziness. Paul's words are sometimes twisted to mean that if people are not eating, they must be unwilling to work. In fact, the vast majority of working-age poor people in our country *are* employed, and most others are either seeking employment or trying to become more employable. Worldwide, it is even more obvious that most hungry people work incredibly hard.

Of course there are poor people who have bad work habits, fail to plan ahead and act irresponsibly. But many prosperous people are self-indulgent, greedy and socially irresponsible. Yet most of us are quicker to judge poor people harshly or to fit them with negative stereotypes. The attitude conveyed in the Bible is far different: there, poor people are respected and their suffering prompts the special concern of God.

The Bible does not, however, take a patronizing view of poor people. Poor people are worthy of respect because they are God's beloved children. They, too, are accountable for their deeds. If a meanness of spirit toward poor people dishonors them, so does a condescending attitude that regards them as blameless or incapable of taking responsibility. These opposites are surprisingly alike, in that both evince little respect for poor people. One judges them, while the other indulges them.

What about biblical texts that assume the persistence of hunger and poverty, such as Jesus' words, "The poor you have always with you"?

If you mean to imply, "So there's no use trying to help," that would clearly fly in the face of Jesus' intention. Jesus made the statement in an unrepeatable situation, when a woman was anointing his feet in a burial ritual on the eve of his crucifixion. The disciples objected that the ointment could have been sold and the proceeds given to the poor. Their protest indicates that Jesus had taught them well, that the needs of the poor were a high priority for them. He indicated as much in this instance: "For you always have the poor with you, and you can show kindness to them whenever you wish . . ." (Mk 14:7). Jesus' comment was drawn from Deuteronomy 15:11, which adds, "I therefore command you, 'Open your hand to the poor and needy neighbor in your land.'" Far from being an excuse for inaction, Jesus' words are a call to costly devotion and relentless care for people in need.

Shouldn't churches take care of the hungry directly? Isn't that the Bible's mandate, rather than working through the government?

Christians could be much more generous. But churches are already doing a lot to take care of hungry people directly. By one estimate, religious congregations give seven billion dollars each year (about one-seventh of their total revenue) to people in need.[3] Christians devote much less effort to influencing what governments do.

God, however, requires both charity and justice, and justice can often be achieved only through the mechanism of government. The view that nations, as well as individuals, will be judged by the way they treat the weakest and most vulnerable among them is deeply embedded in the witness of prophets such as Isaiah, who said:

> How terrible it will be for those who make unfair laws,
>   and those who write laws that make life hard for people.

> They are not fair to the poor,
>   and they rob my people of their rights.
> They allow people to steal from widows
>   and to take from orphans what really belongs to them.
>   *(Is 10:1–2 NCV)*

Jesus criticized and disobeyed laws when they got in the way of helping people. He healed people on the sabbath, for example, even though all work was prohibited on the sabbath. Religion and government were intermixed, so Jesus was challenging the law of the land. The threat Jesus posed to both religious *and* political authorities led to his crucifixion.

Just a few decades ago the segregation of African Americans was strictly enforced in the southern United States and common in the North. Offering charity to victims of segregation was not enough. African Americans needed and insisted on the same civil rights that other citizens enjoyed, a public justice that could only come about through governmental action.

Government is not the only or always the best instrument to deal with hunger. But it is one of the institutions created by God—part of God's providence—for the welfare of people. Because we live in a democracy, a nation with a government "of the people," we have a special privilege and responsibility to use the power of our citizenship to promote public justice and reduce hunger.

But aren't we supposed to maintain a separation between church and state?

Several centuries of religious wars convinced the authors of the U.S. Constitution to protect each person's freedom of religion and prohibit any governmental "establishment of religion." This brilliant feature of the U.S. Constitution has contributed to civil peace in the United States and became even more important as U.S. society grew more diverse.

But most of the founding fathers considered religion important to the morality and health of the nation. Throughout U.S. history, people of faith and religious organizations have often spoken out on political issues. This is part of the "free exercise" of religion that the First Amendment guarantees.

We dare not confuse a proper distinction of roles for church and state with the separation of faith from life. If public policies are relegating people to hunger, Christians have an obligation to speak up for better policies.

Is there a Christian political agenda on hunger?

No, there is no Christian political agenda. The Bible gives us direction, not directives. It is an abomination to God that in a nation as rich as ours many children go hungry. But God has not revealed what kind of system will best help families get into jobs and out of poverty, or what type of safety net to establish for those who otherwise would be left to freeze or starve.

We should respect different points of view. Those who disagree with us frequently have insights we have missed. We need to work with others to find solutions and determine what actually works.

But we dare not use lack of certainty as an excuse for doing nothing. God expects us to make mistakes but does not allow us to turn our backs on those in need.

Is God blaming us for hunger?

It is unlikely that those who read this book purposely cause hunger. But all of us are responsible for reaching out in love and justice to people who are hungry. We have to accept the responsibility—that is, response-ability. Since none of us responds perfectly, each of us bears some measure of guilt, and for that reason we need forgiveness. While guilt often immobilizes us, forgiveness sets us free to try again.

God forgives us, so we are less quick to judge that poor people are simply getting what they deserve. God's grace fills our hearts to overflowing, so we become more compassionate toward others. God feeds us with the Bread of Life and with daily bread, so we are moved to share these gifts with others.

Helping hungry people is to Christian faith as breathing out is to breathing in.

Chapter 3
World Hunger

Decide, mother,
who goes without.
Is it Rama, the strongest,
or Baca, the weakest
Who may not need it much longer
or perhaps Sita?
Who may be expendable?

Decide, mother;
kill a part
of yourself
as you resolve the dilemma.
                    —*Appadura*[1]

Eight hundred twenty-eight million people in developing countries around the world go hungry in the stark sense of lacking enough food to sustain normal activity, according to the most recent estimate of the U.N. Food and Agriculture Organization (FAO). These 828 million people have to survive on fewer calories than their bodies require. They can't live healthy or active lives, and they are highly vulnerable to disease and death.[2]

The World Bank estimates that 1.3 billion people, 20 percent of the human race, live in "absolute poverty."[3] They survive on less than one dollar per day and are too poor to afford an adequate diet and other necessities. If people with deficiencies of micronutrients, such as vitamin A, iron and iodine are also included, the number of hungry people would be closer to two billion.

Hunger hits young children especially hard. Poor nutrition during the first few years of life can result in permanent physical and mental damage, and often death. Of the 31 thousand children under five who die each day in developing countries, about half die from causes related to hunger.[4] That's one child dying for every breath we take.

Has there been progress in reducing world hunger?

Many people imagine that world hunger is a hopeless, immut-able problem. But in fact, the world has made progress toward overcoming hunger.

The *proportion* of people going hungry in developing coun-tries has fallen sharply, from more than one in three in 1970 to one in five by the mid-1990s.[5] The number of hungry people in the developing countries has also declined since the early 1970s, even though the world's total population has increased rapidly.

Progress is not automatic, however. In the early 1990s, the proportion of hungry people continued to decline, but not very rapidly; and the number of hungry people went up slightly. The Asian crisis of the late 1990s is adding to the number of hungry people.

Is progress against world hunger likely to continue?

A study commissioned by the U.S. Agency for International Development (USAID) projected a further decline in the propor-tion of the world's people who are hungry, but a continued increase in the number of hungry people—to 910 million by the year 2015.[6]

A World Food Summit was held in 1996 to follow up the World Food Conference of 1974. At the summit, the nations of the world committed themselves to eliminate half of all hunger by the year 2015—a modest goal compared to Henry Kissinger's 1974 call to end hunger within a decade. But more than a year after the 1996 summit, a U.S. General Accounting Office (GAO) review of the summit process found that the United States and most other governments had made no significant new efforts to achieve the goal they adopted at the summit. As the U.S. gov-ernment developed its food security action plan, it carefully avoided any commitment of additional resources.[7]

What parts of the world have the worst hunger problems?

Sub-Saharan Africa has the highest proportion of hungry people among its population, and hunger is on the increase there. Between 1970 to the mid-1990s the number of hungry people in

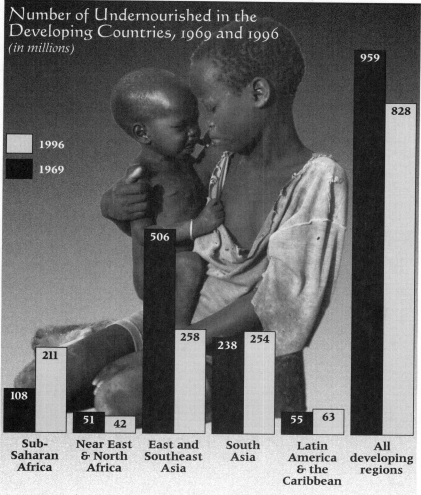

Number of Undernourished in the Developing Countries, 1969 and 1996
(in millions)

1996
1969

	Sub-Saharan Africa	Near East & North Africa	East and Southeast Asia	South Asia	Latin America & the Caribbean	All developing regions
1969	108	51	506	238	55	959
1996	211	42	258	254	63	828

Source: FAO, "Information Note on Estimation of the Number of Undernourished," paper presented at the Committee on World Food Security, Twenty-fourth Session, Rome, 2–5 June 1998.

the region almost doubled, from 108 million to 211 million; and the proportion of hunger in the population decreased from 40 to 39 percent. Per capita food production has been declining in Africa for several decades.

The largest concentration of hungry people is still in South

Asia—Bangladesh, India, Pakistan and Sri Lanka. But the proportion of South Asians who go hungry is decreasing.

East Asia accounted for much of the improvement of the past generation. In China, for example, undernourishment dropped from 45 to 16 percent.[9] But the financial crisis that hit Asia in 1997 has made millions of people hungry again. The World Bank estimates that 20 million people in East Asia fell back into poverty in 1997.[10] The Bank projects that the number of poor people in Indonesia, Thailand, Malaysia and the Philippines may more than double—from 40 million to 100 million[11]—because of the crisis. No one knows how this financial crisis will unfold and what its long-term effects will be.

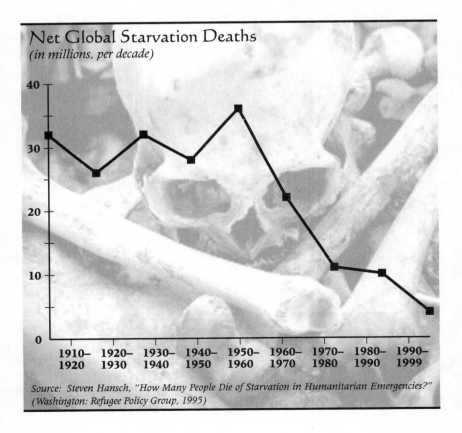

Net Global Starvation Deaths
(in millions, per decade)

Source: Steven Hansch, "How Many People Die of Starvation in Humanitarian Emergencies?" (Washington: Refugee Policy Group, 1995)

In some of the newly independent states of the former Soviet Union hunger has emerged since the collapse of communism. Most countries of the former Soviet Union suffered declines in national income of 40 to 80 percent between 1985 and 1995.[12] Forty percent of the Russian population now lives in poverty.[13] The dismantling of social welfare systems has meant extra hardship for many elderly or otherwise vulnerable people.

How much hunger can be attributed to famine?

Famines are just the tip of the iceberg, responsible for about 3 percent of the approximately seven million hunger-related deaths that occur in a typical year.[14] The vast majority of hunger-related deaths stem from chronic undernutrition, which weakens the body's ability to ward off diseases.

The number of people who die because of famines has dropped sharply during the second half of the twentieth century.

After the Ethiopian famine of the mid-1980s, an international early-warning system was established, so that drought by itself no longer leads to famine. Today's famines are due mainly to tyranny or violence. In North Korea, hundreds of thousands—perhaps millions—of people starved because of the dictatorship's failed economic policies and isolation. In the Sudan, civil war causes famine.

What causes most hunger?

People go hungry because they are extremely poor. They neither produce enough food for their families nor can they afford to buy what they need.

Typically, people that poor also feel powerless. In developing countries they are usually illiterate. The life they have experienced is one of extreme hardship. They may live in a harsh climate, own little or no land, and have no access to decision makers, who readily ignore them. If they are women, children, ethnic minorities or at the bottom end of a caste system, they are even more vulnerable. Their powerlessness is not just a subjective feeling. But it is not only an objective reality, either. The perception they have of their powerlessness becomes self-fulfilling. So changing that perception—becoming aware of possible oppor-

tunities to improve life, such as joining a literacy class or participating in a development project, can be the first step away from
hunger and poverty.

The causes of the poverty that lies behind hunger are many.
The inherited circumstances of countries and of people within
countries reflect vast differences. Their histories and traditions
are an unequal mixture of strengths and weaknesses, assets and
liabilities. These, along with the climate, geography and natural
resources they have, do not give all people the same opportunities. On the contrary, the playing field is exceedingly uneven. At
the same time, some countries with few advantages outperform
others that are more favorably endowed. It is possible to learn
from both successes and failures how hunger and poverty can be
overcome, as the subsequent chapters will attempt to show.

Can you help me imagine what life is like for hungry people?

Here is a snapshot of three of the developing world's 828 million
hungry people:

- Malekha Khatun, a landless mother in Bangladesh
- Gabriella Lautaru, a child growing up on the streets of
  Rumania
- Ricardo Cabrera, a Honduran coffee farmer.

Malekha Khatun was born in the village of Dhemsha in
Bangladesh. She lost her father, the family's wage earner, when
she was young. Malekha, her younger brother and her mother
had no house and slept outside. In this wet climate, they got
soaked when it rained unless someone else offered shelter. Her
childhood was spent helping her mother earn money. She also
attended school for a few years. Her brother died from fever
when he was nine.

At fourteen, Malekha was married off to a man from
another village. Malekha became pregnant right away. She
moved in with her husband's family when he left to work as a
menial laborer so that he could send money back to her and the
baby. Soon after he returned, she got pregnant again. When

Malekha's husband left a second time, she received no money or word from him. She was on her own with two small children and no means of income. Her youngest child died of malnutrition and diarrhea.

Malekha worked at various jobs, becoming skilled at knitting and making nets. She moved from her husband's family's home to live with her mother. Hard work and resourcefulness enabled her to run a small grocery store, but competition caused her business to suffer, and she sometimes had to fall back on begging.

Malekha's constant hard work and industriousness could not overcome the poverty and hunger that shadow a woman alone on the bottom rung of a poor nation. For all her struggling, Malekha ended up with no food to feed herself, no umbrella to protect her from the rain and only one sari to her name.[15]

A world away, in Bucharest, Rumania, Gabriella Lautaru, five years old, lives with her brother Dumitre, eleven years old, in a sewer. They sniff glue to numb the hunger and cold they face each day.

Malnutrition and squalor mark the lives of an army of street children and orphans in Bucharest. A harsh and clumsy communist dictatorship, followed by a chaotic transition to free markets, has caused massive economic hardship. Gabriella and Dumitre's parents died. Many children are abandoned.

"I know it's bad that Gabriella sniffs glue, but what can I do?" Dumitre says. "I would give anything if my sister didn't have to live here."[16]

In still another part of the world, Ricardo Cabrera, his wife and his seven children live in a small hut in Marcala, Honduras. Cabrera sums up his life: "Yes, I am a poor man. *Bastante, bastante, bastante* [a lot, a lot, a lot]." To provide a meager living for his family, he works hard in the fields, along with his children. Half the year he works for the large landowners, and half the year he grows food for his family and coffee to sell on his own farm.

Ricardo says, "At the time I was born, people in the mountains were dying of hunger. I had three brothers and a sister; two brothers died of fever. My parents worked from six in the morning to six in the evening. It's the rich who don't work."

When he was twenty-one and newly married, Ricardo was drafted into the army. After taxes and money for food, clothes and medicine were subtracted from his pay, he had only twenty-five cents a month to send home to his new wife. He has worked hard to get to where he is today, though he is still, as he says, a poor man.

"Make no mistake," Ricardo says. "My people and I don't want any sweet music. We want our children to be educated, we want to know how to farm better. We don't want to be cheated."[17]

Chapter 4

Hunger Next Door

I was in the food pantry with a young man and his son who had come needing help with some groceries. I like to chat with folks to set them at ease while I fix the food baskets—just general conversation to put us on the same level and break down some of the walls that divide us. But I was having a difficult time talking to this gentleman. He seemed especially uncomfortable, very stiff, keeping his hands tucked inside his coat pockets. Finally, he thrust out his balled-up fist.

"Here is some money that I found on the floor outside the pantry," *he said as he handed over about $20 in rolled up bills. "Does it belong to you?"*

I assured him that it didn't and told him that since he found it, he should just keep it.

"No, I am certain that this belongs to you," he insisted.

I repeated that I was sure it didn't and again urged him to keep the money for his family.

"You don't understand," he said haltingly as his voice cracked a bit. Putting his arm around his son, he told me, "This is really hard for me. I have never had to ask for help before. I own my own rig and drive for a living. We usually do real good, but there just hasn't been any work and I have to do something to feed my family. I want you to give this money to help someone else."

I was stunned. After all, the food we were giving him probably wouldn't have cost us more than $35 wholesale. I was about to launch into my usual line, reassuring him that everybody needs help now and again. . . . Then it hit me.

He was using this incredibly difficult moment as an opportunity to teach his son, and here I was about to blow it. It made me stop for a minute and think about this man as an individual. Too often, I realized, I just moved through my day of helping others so quickly and so convinced that I had heard it all before. But no one is simply another "client." Each of us is a child of God and each has a right to be here.

So, I thanked him. And I did use his gift later that day to help get food for another family. The real gift he gave me will always stay with me, though.

—Rob Ercoline,
Little Flower Catholic Church,
South Bend, Indiana

How widespread is hunger in the United States?

In 1997 the U.S. government released the first-ever official data on hunger and food security in the United States.[1] It was based on 45 thousand Census Bureau household interviews in 1995. The survey used these definitions:

- *Food insecurity*—a household in which adjustments in food management, including reduced quality of diets, have occurred;

- *Moderate hunger*—a household in which adults have reduced their food intake and repeatedly experienced the uneasy or painful sensation of hunger;

- *Severe hunger*—a household in which children's intake of food has been reduced enough to make them repeatedly experience the uneasy or painful sensation of hunger, and where adults have experienced more extensive reductions in food intake.

The survey found that 35 million people (one out of every eight) live in U.S. households that are food insecure or hungry. Eleven million people live in households that suffer severe or moderate hunger, and two million of those are in households that suffer severe hunger.

In a separate exercise, the Department of Agriculture estimated that roughly 3 percent of the U.S. population—about seven million people—are hungry according to the definition which the Food and Agriculture Organization (FAO) uses in developing countries. Their food intake regularly deprives them of enough calories.[2]

Prevalence of Household Food Security and Hunger

Food Insecure with Severe Hunger — 0.8% or 2 million people

Food Insecure with Hunger — 3.3% or 9 million people

Food Insecure without Hunger — 7.8% or 24 million people

Food Secure 88% of households

Food Insecure 12% of households or 35 million people

Source: U.S. Department of Agriculture

What sorts of people go hungry in the United States?

If we visit some of the 35 million people in food insecure or hungry households, we find that they aren't much different from the rest of us—just a lot poorer. We meet an older wife and husband who have worked hard their entire lives only to find their savings wiped out by medical bills. We see a child sneaking food from a friend's kitchen cabinet as they play together after school.

We see an addicted woman who can't keep a job or take good care of her children. There's another woman and her daughter—both struggling with mental illness and unable to make themselves leave their apartment, much less hold down jobs. We meet a single mother who has to choose whether the income from her minimum wage job will go to pay rent or buy groceries.

What are the main causes of hunger in the United States?

Here, as elsewhere, people go hungry because they are poor. And, as elsewhere, powerlessness is also a factor. Poor people usually don't have much education and sometimes feel beaten down by years of failure and frustration. Most poor people don't vote.

Because hunger everywhere is driven by poverty, it is not surprising that the number of people in food insecure households (35 million) is about the same as the number of those living in poverty (36 million).[3] In fact, the official U.S. poverty line is *defined* by how much income it takes to purchase a minimally adequate diet.[4]

What, then, is the picture of poverty in our country?

In 1997, 13 percent of the U.S. population (36 million people) fell below the official poverty line. If we include non-cash government support, such as food stamps and Medicaid, 10 percent of the U.S. population (27 million people) fell below the poverty line.[5]

Thirty percent of the U.S. population fell below the poverty line for at least two months during the three-year period from 1993–95. The average amount of time spent in poverty was four and a half months. Most did not live in constant and habitual poverty, but were buffeted temporarily by circumstances. Only 13 percent of those who experienced poverty were poor for more than two years.[6] For many poverty is a revolving door; but for some it is a trap door.

African Americans, Hispanics, and Native Americans have far higher rates of poverty than the nation as a whole. Women, especially unmarried women with children, are more frequently poor than men. High school dropouts and children of single parents also face a much higher incidence of poverty. Eleven percent of the elderly (age sixty-five and over) are poor; the elderly used to be the poorest age group, but now are less poor than the U.S. population as a whole, thanks in part to programs such as Social Security and Medicare.[7]

Poor people in developing countries are typically much poorer, in material terms, than poor people in the United States. However, because poor people in this country are surrounded by affluence, constantly reminded of their failure to share fully in the American dream and often made to feel morally culpable, the emotional impact of poverty can be a greater burden here.

Have hunger and poverty been on the increase in the United States?

The U.S. government just recently began gathering data on hunger and food insecurity. But the dramatic growth of private charitable feeding efforts since the late 1970s suggests growing hunger. As many churches and synagogues found more people coming in off the streets for help buying groceries, they banded together to form neighborhood food pantries, soup kitchens and then food banks. There were few such organizations in 1980, but an estimated 150 thousand private feeding agencies are now passing out food to hungry Americans.[8]

The United States has maintained data on poverty over time, and the graph on the next page tells a disappointing story. The number and proportion of the U.S. population in poverty dropped from 1959 to the mid-1970s. The rapid economic growth of that period acted, in the words of John F. Kennedy, like a rising tide that "lifts all boats." The expansion of food stamps and other anti-poverty programs during the Johnson and Nixon administrations further reduced hunger. Then the economy slowed and programs were cut.

The economy also changed. The wages of low-skill workers have lagged behind inflation since the late 1970s, as the importance of knowledge and technology, together with international competition increased.

Declining real wages among low-skill workers is a major reason for growing poverty and hunger. Overall population growth, immigration and the increase in single-parent families also added to the number of people who are poor.

In 1997, 13 percent of the population was poor, up from 11

Number of Poor and Poverty Rate in the United States, 1959–1997
(numbers in millions)

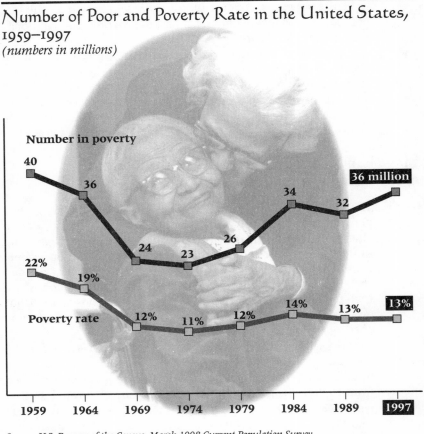

Source: U.S. Bureau of the Census, March 1998 Current Population Survey.

percent in 1974. The number of people in poverty swelled from 23 million to 36 million. Poverty dropped a bit in the late 1990s, mainly because a long period of economic expansion was finally improving the job market for everybody; but growth doesn't reduce unemployment or poverty as much as it used to do.

The poverty figures in the graph do not take account of non-cash assistance programs, such as food stamps. Food stamps and some other assistance programs were scaled back after 1996. That's part of the reason why Catholic Charities, Lutheran Services of America, the Salvation Army and other assistance networks all reported sharp increases in requests for emergency food in the late 1990s, a sign of growing hunger in the midst of a booming economy.[9] Catholic Charities reported a 26 percent increase between June 1997 and April 1998.[10] The U.S. Conference of Mayors reported a 14 percent increase in requests for emergency assistance in 1998, and said that 21 percent of all requests went unmet.[11]

Welfare reform was also pushing some people into low-wage jobs. Second Harvest reported that most of the people coming to food pantries and soup kitchens for the first time in 1997 had jobs, but at low wages and without health insurance. Many employed people were not making enough money to make ends meet.

So the short answer is: yes, hunger and poverty have been on the increase in the United States.

How does the United States compare to other countries at about the same level of income?

All the industrial countries have experienced sluggish demand for unskilled labor. It shows up in low wages in the United States and as high unemployment in the more regulated economies of western Europe.

Western Europe and Canada have more extensive social welfare systems than the United States. They have cut back on social programs somewhat in the 1980s and 1990s, and that has resulted in more poverty—and sometimes hunger—than before. But their social welfare systems are still more extensive and hunger among their people less prevalent.

The percentage of children in poverty in the United States is triple the average for the other industrial nations. In the other industrial countries, governments provide far more assistance to poor children.[12]

How are U.S. children affected by hunger and poverty?

One child in five lives in poverty. One child in five lives in a food-insecure household.[13]

Child Poverty in Industrial Countries

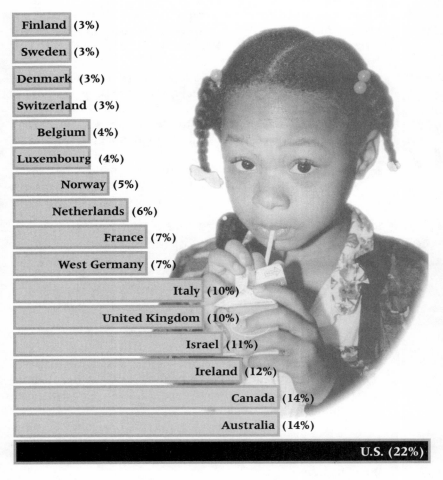

Finland (3%)

Sweden (3%)

Denmark (3%)

Switzerland (3%)

Belgium (4%)

Luxembourg (4%)

Norway (5%)

Netherlands (6%)

France (7%)

West Germany (7%)

Italy (10%)

United Kingdom (10%)

Israel (11%)

Ireland (12%)

Canada (14%)

Australia (14%)

U.S. (22%)

Source: Luxembourg Income Study

How Much Government Transfers Reduce Child Poverty

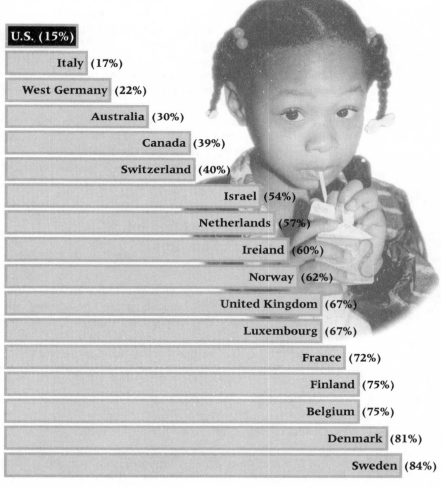

U.S. (15%)

Italy (17%)

West Germany (22%)

Australia (30%)

Canada (39%)

Switzerland (40%)

Israel (54%)

Netherlands (57%)

Ireland (60%)

Norway (62%)

United Kingdom (67%)

Luxembourg (67%)

France (72%)

Finland (75%)

Belgium (75%)

Denmark (81%)

Sweden (84%)

Source: Luxembourg Income Study

Poverty is even more widespread among very young children. One in four U.S. children five years old or younger lives in poverty.[14]

Even mild undernutrition—the kind seen widely in the United States—produces cognitive impairments in children that can last a lifetime, according to J. Larry Brown, director of the Center on Hunger, Poverty and Nutrition Policy at Tufts University. When children don't eat enough, they become less alert—less engaged with their environment, less able to pay attention to parents and teachers.[15]

Poor children are more likely to become unmarried teen parents, drop out of school and commit violent crimes. They are less likely to grow into constructive adults. Ultimately we all pay a high price for this—a far higher price than the cost of reducing hunger and poverty. Far better to offer them a place at the table!

How much of Bread for the World's work is devoted to world hunger and how much to hunger in the United States?

Bread for the World has always worked on both international and domestic hunger. Hunger in our midst can't be ignored, but compassion doesn't stop at the border. Over the years, Bread for the World has devoted most of its efforts to world hunger issues. The scale and intensity of hunger in the developing world are compelling, and few other U.S. voices speak up for hungry people overseas.

In the 1990s, however, Bread for the World has probably devoted about half of its overall effort to hunger in the United States. This increased emphasis on domestic hunger responds to the fact that U.S. hunger has increased, while hunger worldwide has declined. In addition, the ongoing process of welfare reform is a *major* shift in U.S. policy toward poor and hungry people in our country. Developing-country policies toward poor people are powerfully influenced by what they see the United States do domestically.

Furthermore, it may be impossible to win more considerate U.S. policies toward hungry people in Africa or Asia as long as our political leaders remain as distracted from the problems of hungry people in our own nation, as they now are. The political movement needed to win action against hunger at home and abroad would draw most of its energy from people's concern about hunger in their own communities.

Can you bring this down to earth again by talking about a few people who go hungry in our country?

Members of the Hunger Action Leadership Team of Tampa Bay, Florida—who live in a low-income neighborhood—interviewed hungry people in their community. The Hunger Action Leadership Team has been part of a Bread for the World Institute leadership development program. Here are snippets of what they heard from several of their neighbors.[16]

My name is Katheren. I'm thirty-five years old. My husband is forty-two years old. I have two sons eight and nine. I am a white female, blond, like working with animals. My husband is not the father of the boys. He has a slight mental problem.

Sometimes I have problems feeding my family. There's not enough food at the end of the month. We don't have enough money many times to drive to where the bargains are.

The kinds of help we're getting now are food stamps, Medicaid, donated food from the food bank and other resources. I'd like to complete my education, to get a decent job so I won't need food stamps.

There are six of us in our household, ages thirty-two, thirty-three, twenty, eight, seven and four. Mom prepares all the meals, and our favorite foods are Mexican. Our usual breakfast is eggs, milk and beans. For lunch we have tortillas and meat, and the same for dinner. We eat our meals outside the trailer.

We do have trouble feeding our family sometimes. We have hard times during the time of the year when there is no work. We get through them by getting help from family and friends. We have run out of food, and we asked for help from the churches.

Our biggest problem is finding a safe, inexpensive place to leave our children. The one thing we would change to make our lives better is to go to school so we can have better opportunities.

There are four persons in our household. Our ages are thirty, eight, eight months, and eighty-five. We're not picky about the food we eat.

My elderly aunt is diabetic. She eats in her bed. Because I am taking care of my sick aunt, I can't work.

Do I ever have problems feeding my family? Yes, because we don't have enough food. We get food stamps and donations of food now. It would help us if we had coupons so we could get discounts. Also, more available donations of food, especially for diabetics. We are going through hard times right now.

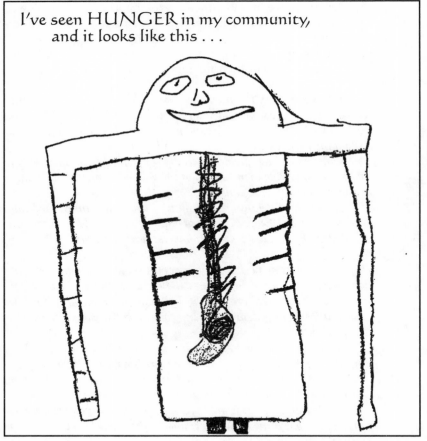

I've seen HUNGER in my community, and it looks like this . . .

Jeremy Leroy, Age eleven
Clearwater, Florida

Section 11

Ending Hunger

Chapter 5
Focused Efforts

> One woman [in El Salvador], who is eighty years old, tells us, "The one thing I want to see before I die is clean water at my house." She and other members of the community have been walking an hour each time they need water—and paying a large sum for it. When asked what she will do with the savings, one mother says, "I could buy more food for my children and then my family will be healthier."[1]

Tested, inexpensive solutions to hunger are available. What's missing is the political will to extend them more widely.

This chapter looks at two child survival programs—one in developing countries and one in the United States. The first program saves the lives of millions of children around the world each year. In 1960, nearly one child in five died before his or her fifth birthday in developing countries. Now it's one child in nine.[2] Much of this amazing improvement can be attributed to child survival efforts. The second program has improved nutrition for millions of infants and small children in the United States. Although the effectiveness of these two approaches is widely acknowledged across party lines, getting the U.S. government to support them has required dogged citizen action.

What are these child survival programs?

Most of the children who die from hunger actually die from a combination of malnutrition and disease. Beginning in the mid-1980s, UNICEF urged the widespread promotion of four simple techniques to improve child nutrition and health. Recent advances in mass media and communications, along with nationwide community mobilizations, have enabled developing countries to disseminate these four approaches widely, even in poor and remote regions.

- *Growth monitoring.* Simple systems can check if children have normal weight and measurements and, if not, help the parents provide better nutrition. In Indonesia, for example, a nationwide women's organization took responsibility for checking monthly, village by village, whether all the children in the village showed healthy growth. A visiting nurse could use that data to spot undernutrition in children. The parents of those children were alerted, taught about nutrition and helped with fresh vegetables.
- *Oral rehydration therapy.* Two million children in developing countries die each year from dehydration brought on by severe and prolonged bouts of diarrhea. A child's body may be weakened by malnutrition, and the cause of diarrhea may be unclean water or a lack of sanitary facilities. But it's often diarrheal dehydration that kills.[3] A solution of sugar and salt in clean water (oral rehydration) has saved millions of children's lives. The solution helps the dehydrated body absorb fluids quickly. UNICEF and others sell packets of sugar and salt that cost about ten cents each, and parents can be taught to make the formula themselves.
- *Breast feeding.* In the 1950s and 1960s, many mothers around the world switched from nursing their children to using baby formula, partly in response to commercial marketing. But formula isn't as healthful as mother's milk, especially when the formula is prepared under unsanitary conditions. Religious and other groups around the world campaigned to curb misleading advertisements for baby food in developing countries, and health officials finally joined them in mass education about breast feeding. Worldwide reduction of formula feeding and improved breast-feeding practices may be saving 1.5 million children a year.[4]
- *Immunization.* By the mid-1980s, a vaccine had been developed that could protect children from seven diseases at once. Developing countries across the globe initiated all-out vaccination campaigns, and by the end of the decade, most countries had achieved 80 percent immunization rates. These rates have been sustained, saving three million lives each year.[5]

Since the campaign for child survival was launched, other features have been added to these four basic methods. One is the promotion of micronutrients: vitamins and minerals that, in tiny amounts and at very low cost, can make a great difference in children's health. Millions have gone blind for lack of vitamin A, but vitamin A deficiency contributes even more widely to children's deaths—two every minute, UNICEF reported in 1995. Consequently improved diets, fortified foods and the distribution of two-cent tablets have become part of the children's health and survival campaign. The lack of iodine causes mental retardation, so this, too, has been added to the arsenal of inexpensive initiatives.

Child survival programs have played a big role in dramatically reducing the death rate of children five and under in developing countries. The HIV epidemic could stall or even reverse some of this progress, but the achievement of the child survival revolution is nevertheless extraordinary.

What lessons can we draw from these efforts?

The most telling lesson has been about winning political support. James P. Grant, the head of UNICEF from 1980 until his death in 1995, is a hero. He relentlessly promoted child survival programs to grass-roots groups, Washington politicians and heads of state. On three separate occasions in 1985, Grant convinced both sides in El Salvador's bloody civil war to stop fighting for a day so that 20 thousand health care workers could immunize a quarter million children.[6] More broadly, millions of citizens in developing countries, along with their governments, media, churches and schools, mobilized massive national campaigns to get the job done.

Promoting child survival in the midst of El Salvador's civil war was tough, but winning support from the U.S. Congress took even more effort. In 1985 Bread for the World drafted legislation that established a Child Survival Fund within the U.S. Agency for International Development (USAID). Congress approved the fund with an initial appropriation of $25 million.

In 1986 Bread for the World, together with Results (another grass-roots lobby on hunger issues), pushed to expand the Child Survival Fund. They urged that Congress increase the annual allocation by $50 million. By mid-summer of that year, more than half of the members of the House of Representatives had cosponsored the legislation. The appropriations subcommittee that deals with funding levels for foreign aid programs recommended a $25 million increase.

1986 was the first year of the Gramm-Rudmann Budget Reduction Act, passed by Congress to impose strict limits on spending in the face of a ballooning federal deficit. Advocates for the Child Survival Fund were told by aides to members of Congress that the fund was lucky to get any increase at all and its backers shouldn't rock the boat. Nevertheless, Bread for the World and Results fought for the full $50 million increase and won.

At the time, UNICEF estimated that it cost five dollars to fully immunize a child against the major vaccine preventable diseases. The additional $50 million provided the money to immunize ten million children, which by UNICEF's estimate saved 125 thousand lives.

By 1998, U.S. foreign aid funding for the child survival program had reached $300 million a year. In addition, the United States had substantially increased funding for child survival activities through UNICEF and other programs. This commitment on the part of the U.S. government has played a big role in saving the lives of millions of young children.

Is the domestic child nutrition program that you mentioned similar?

The Special Supplemental Nutrition Program for Women, Infants and Children (WIC) provides additional food, nutrition education and/or medical screening to low-income pregnant women, new mothers, infants and children up to age five—when the funds are available.

Research has confirmed what WIC mothers know from their own experience: WIC works. This program reduces infant mortality and anemia, and it increases cognitive performance in children. Research published in the *Journal of Nutrition* in March 1998, found that preschool-aged children in the WIC program have healthier diets than other children in low-income families.[7] In addition WIC gives participants lifelong nutrition skills.

A study by Mathematica Policy Research in 1993 showed that WIC reduces infant mortality. The rates of reduction in infant deaths in WIC programs studied varied from 25 to 66 percent.[8]

But WIC not only saves lives, it saves money. A study conducted by the U.S. General Accounting Office found that women receiving Medicaid and prenatal WIC services had substantially lower rates of low-birth-weight babies than women who received Medicaid but no prenatal WIC. Every dollar invested in pregnant women in WIC produced $1.91 to $4.21 in Medicaid savings for newborns and their mothers.[9] Putting low-birth-weight babies in intensive care is much more expensive than helping pregnant women buy groceries.

The long-term effects of WIC are suggested by a remarkable study, published in the *Journal of the American Medical Association*. It did not study WIC, but did document the long-term effects of nursing care for pregnant women and new mothers, which is one element of WIC. The researchers focused on single, low-income mothers and went back to find out how their children were doing 15 years later.

Adolescents born to women who received nurse visits before and after their births—15 years before—reported fewer instances of running away from home, fewer arrests, fewer convictions and violations of probation, fewer lifetime sex partners, fewer cigarettes smoked per day and less use of alcohol.[10]

What has Bread for the World done for WIC?

WIC began 25 years ago. Bread for the World has consistently worked to build bipartisan support for the program. Over the years, its main annual campaign has periodically focused on WIC, and the program has gradually expanded.

Mary Helene Mele, a Bread for the World member from Arlington, Virginia, recalls her first lobbying effort for WIC, in 1987. One day, as she was drinking a glass of water in preparation for an afternoon jog, a Bread for the World newsletter article on WIC caught her eye:

I read . . . the BFW explanation of WIC (of which I had never heard) and the importance of getting increased funding for this program. I remember to this day how the study had shown that WIC saved money in public health costs down the road. Well-fed women have healthier babies. Made sense.

I then jogged to the library and returned some books, and noticed on the bulletin board that our representative was going to be at the post office to meet with constituents. I had never met my representative—or any member of Congress for that matter—and jogging to the post office and home would be a nice run. I worried about appearing hot and sweaty in my jogging shorts. But then I thought there would probably be quite a crowd of people, and I could keep to the rear, see what he looked like, hear what he had to say and then go home unnoticed.

But things did not go as Mele expected.

I arrived at the post office—and there he was, as promised. And there was no one else. Just me and the Congressman, an aide at his side and the postal employees behind the counter. He looked up at me as I came in. I went white with fear inside and I thought, for hungry women and children, go talk to him.

I asked him if he would support increased funding for WIC. I was articulate; it must have been the Holy Spirit. He was attentive.

I called his office the following week. He had committed to supporting increased funding for WIC. I forget the numbers now, but at the time I figured out that if I fed the homeless for every night of the week for the rest of my life, I might not have given as much as I did that ten minutes in the post office.

Mele's representative, Frank Wolf, did support Bread for the World's initiative. So did more than half the members of the House and the Senate. That year Congress appropriated a $73 million increase in WIC, enough to provide benefits to about 150 thousand more mothers and small children. Representative Wolf gradually became a key leader among House Republicans on hunger issues.

As of 1998, 82 percent of the eligible women, infants and children were able to participate in WIC, up from 42 percent in 1987. But Congress had slowed its efforts to expand WIC.

Doesn't this show that there *is* growing political support against hunger?

It shows that personal efforts to push for action on specific legislation make a big difference. At the same time, after all these years of impressive gains against hunger and infant mortality, why is there still not enough funding so that all the mothers and small children who qualify for WIC can benefit? Why does Congress now resist extending WIC to all the mothers and small children who qualify for WIC? And why are child survival activities not expanded even further in developing countries? These are two well-known, popular programs, so not many members of Congress oppose either. However, competing uses of government money get higher priority. It's a question of what's most important to politicians, which interests lobby most effectively and what the voters back home insist on.

These are just two examples of focused approaches that could readily be expanded to reduce hunger. There are other proven approaches that are underutilized. For example, microcredit (lending small amounts of money to poor people so they can start their own businesses) has lifted millions of people out of poverty in developing countries. In the United States, the Earned Income Tax Credit has helped millions of low-income working families make ends meet by giving tax breaks to working poor people. Agricultural research and training help small-scale farmers in the developing world increase their food production and incomes. The installation of water pipes and pit latrines curtails the spread of deadly diseases that prey on malnourished children in poorer nations. The list goes on.

As the history of child survival programs and WIC demonstrates, the United States lacks the political will to fully implement even some of the most effective, least controversial initiatives to reduce hunger.

Chapter 6

The Way Out

"Sir, I'm hungry!" pleaded a five-year-old boy in Addis Ababa, Ethiopia.

He had approached Bernard Confer and Leslie Weber, Lutheran executives engaged in relief and development work. They turned, and as Weber tells it, "I had no doubt about his being hungry. He wore a single cloth garment and his eyes bulged. I reached in my pocket and gave him a coin. Soon there were other children and my Ethiopian money was gone. My friend Confer said, "You have helped these children today, but who will help them tomorrow?"

Who will help them tomorrow?

Or to ask the question underlying that one: How can we deal with the *causes* of hunger? What are the long-range solutions?

Special programs to reduce hunger, like child survival and WIC, have yielded impressive results, but most of the world's progress against hunger has been due to broad-based economic and social development. When people go hungry, it's a sign that many things have gone wrong, just as reductions in hunger usually signal that society as a whole is becoming healthier. *Broad-based economic growth, focused efforts to reduce poverty, environmental protection* and *democracy* are key elements of a development strategy that can overcome widespread hunger.

How much does economic growth contribute to reducing hunger?

Growth is an essential part of the solution. The Industrial Revolution launched a long period of increasing incomes, especially in Europe and North America. After World War II, countries in Latin America, Asia and Africa began to modernize with the aim of attaining a higher standard of living. As countries achieved political independence, they intensified their economic efforts.

Average income per capita in the developing countries in 1995 was two-and-a-half times what it was in 1960.[1] The experience among countries was very uneven, however. Many developing countries, especially in Africa, grew little or even regressed. But others, mainly in East Asia, Southern Europe and the Middle East, achieved a period of sustained and rapid growth without precedent. This expansion allowed millions of families to work their way out of poverty. The financial problems of some developing countries in the late 1990s have not reversed all these gains.

Poor people have done best when the pattern of economic growth opened opportunities to low-income groups. In some countries, such as Brazil, or the United States since the mid-1970s, high-income groups have benefited most from economic growth. But Southeast Asian nations invested heavily in rural roads and agricultural development. Because most of the poorest people live in rural areas, they were able to increase their earnings. An orientation toward exports helped, too, because export industries in developing countries are labor intensive and generate lots of jobs. In Malaysia, a massive program of affirmative action allowed the largest and poorest ethnic group to take part in the economic expansion.

How important are targeted efforts to reduce poverty and hunger?

Nearly all developing countries—even those that have not achieved economic growth—have promoted child survival techniques and strengthened systems of basic health care and sanitation. As a result, child mortality has declined dramatically almost everywhere. Average life expectancy in developing nations increased from 46 years in 1960 to 62 in 1995.

Virtually all developing countries have also invested heavily in education. Primary school enrollment has gone up, and adult literacy also improved sharply, climbing from 48 percent in 1970 to 70 percent by 1995.[2]

The dynamic economies of East Asia combined economic growth with focused efforts to meet everybody's fundamental needs for health care, basic education, sufficient food, drinkable water and adequate shelter. Helping disadvantaged people is the

Child Mortality Rate, 1960–1997
(per 1,000 live births in developing countries)

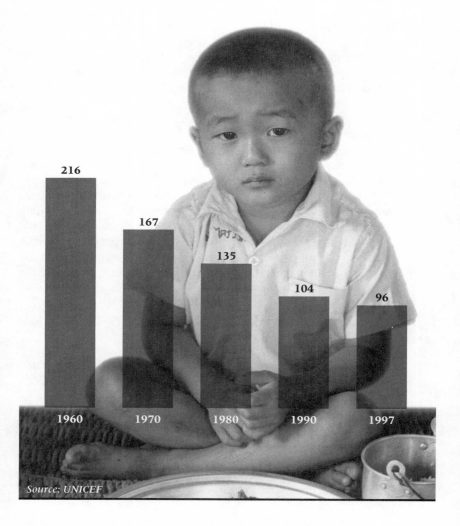

216

167

135

104

96

1960   1970   1980   1990   1997

Source: UNICEF

right thing to do, but it also turns out to be a smart national investment. People who are healthy, literate and well fed can contribute more to the economy and cultural life.

Won't the drive for economic and social progress in developing countries be held back by environmental problems?

Environmental protection is crucial to sustained reduction in poverty and hunger.

Past environmental neglect now adds to Southeast Asia's problems. The damage that multinational timber companies and poor farmers have done to Indonesia's rain forests led to massive, runaway forest fires in 1997.[3] In large Asian cities many people have to wear masks because of air pollution. Environmental excesses ultimately must be paid for, and poor people often suffer the effects of environmental destruction.

Many of the world's poorest people live in fragile environments—on dry lands, in mountainous areas, near rain forests. Commercial development and population growth are straining these environments. As a result, many people are losing the resources on which their meager livelihoods depend. In these situations, reducing hunger clearly depends on patterns of economic development that protect natural resources.

If economic growth, focused efforts to reduce poverty and environmental protection are important to reducing hunger, what about democracy?

Democracy also contributes to ending hunger, especially when poor people have a say in decisions that affect them.

Amartya Sen, who won a Nobel prize in economics for his work on hunger and poverty, demonstrated that there are almost never famines in democratic countries. A free press and popular agitation compel national and international action as food becomes scarce. But dictators have other priorities, may not want to acknowledge the shortcomings of their regimes and can keep the press at bay.[4]

Democracy doesn't guarantee justice for poor people, of course. The majority may not vote for policies that would help poor people, and poor people themselves can sometimes be swayed by populist politicians with ill-advised quick fixes. But the nations that have been democracies longest (western Europe and North America) are also among the most prosperous and have all made substantial efforts to promote social welfare.

During the last two decades and thanks to tremendous grassroots struggles, many nations have moved toward democracy. As late as 1988, only 66 of the world's nations were democracies. By 1998, that number had risen to 117.[5]

As new and often struggling democracies have dealt with economic problems, they seem to have protected vulnerable people more than the dictators of the past. The current prevalence of democracy helps to make this an opportune time for progress against hunger.

It's especially important that low-income people get organized and speak up for themselves. When people of modest means have organized themselves—as the U.S. labor union movement did early in this century—they have been able to win important gains.

Some private agencies that help poor communities in developing countries have worked for decades to build the capacity of low-income people and communities to make decisions for themselves and push for change. This has been a core activity for church agencies such as Church World Service, Lutheran World Relief and Catholic Relief Services. More recently, some governments and official aid services have begun trying to work in ways that support local participation in decision making and local management.

Is there reason to be optimistic about the prospects of ending most hunger?

Hope may be a better stance than optimism.

- The world has already made significant progress against hunger.
- The world has learned from experience what works.
- This is a period of relative peace and prosperity.
- People around the globe have demanded and obtained more democratic government.
- People everywhere are insisting on environmental care.

What's missing is a similar wave of insistence that parallel steps be taken to overcome widespread hunger and human deprivation.

The United States could lead an international effort to overcome world hunger. Coauthor David Beckmann wrote speeches for the president of the World Bank during the first years of the international debt crisis in the 1980s and watched up-close how the U.S. government often sets policy for the world. The United States, represented by its secretary of the treasury, James Baker, proposed a very limited response to the debt crisis. The other industrial countries agreed to the Baker Plan; the World Bank and IMF implemented it; and most developing countries had no choice but to struggle along the lines that the United States urged. As a result, tens of millions of vulnerable people went hungry.

After several years, a different secretary of the treasury, Nicholas Brady, called for a slightly more generous response. Again, other governments agreed, the World Bank and IMF preached the new doctrine, and that's what people in the indebted countries had to live with. The Brady Plan helped some countries restore economic growth, so their debt became more manageable. For many of the poorest developing countries, however, the Brady Plan offered too little help. Some of these countries have yet to recover from the debt crisis of the early 1980s.

Just as the United States has set the pace (a slow pace) of response to the debt problems of poor countries, a U.S. commitment to overcome hunger in the world would elicit commitments from many other governments in both the industrial and developing countries. Within that framework, low-income communities, businesses and religious and civic groups throughout the world would also undertake new initiatives to overcome hunger.

What is the path to reduced hunger in the United States?

The same four elements of healthy development are also relevant in the United States. Economic growth is essential to hungry and poor people in this country. The poverty rate goes up when the economy slows down.

But the United States can learn from successfully developing countries to invest in *all* its people. The United States invests a lower share of its national income in basic education and health for low-income people than many other countries. The United States is less successful than some developing countries in immunizing all children, and infant mortality rates are higher in the nation's capital, for example, than in Costa Rica and Cuba.[6] All other industrial countries maintain more extensive social welfare programs.

Increased investment in health, education and nutrition would reduce hunger directly and also help U.S. workers participate fully in economic growth. If the United States fails to invest more in all its people, the U.S. economy and society will become more and more polarized.

Environmental protection also applies to the United States, which has made some progress toward environmental sustainability but still has a long way to go. U.S. patterns of production and consumption put tremendous strains on the environment, and low-income communities often take the brunt of environmental damage—from waste dumps on the poor side of town to strip mines in Appalachia.

The United States is blessed with strong democratic institutions. Citizens have real influence, when they choose to use it. Yet the number of U.S. citizens who don't vote keeps rising; and even among those who do vote, relatively few ever write their members of Congress in support of legislation for the common good.

Democracy can be a powerful tool for reducing hunger in the United States and worldwide. U.S. citizens have real power. That power is a gift from God and should be used to help end hunger in God's world.

Section III

The Overloaded Earth

Chapter 7

You Can't Save Forests
If People Are Starving

The whine of Jose Carvalho's chain saw pierces the humid stillness of the Amazon rain forest. As birds scatter from the canopy high overhead, the saw gnaws at the trunk of a towering tree, which soon falls with a loud crack. Jose is cutting down the tree to guarantee food on the table and a livelihood for his family of six, which lives in one of the least hospitable places in the world. Torrential rains make life miserable during the wet season. Malaria strikes repeatedly, weakening Jose and his family and leaving them vulnerable to the ravages of hunger.

Although Jose grows rice, beans and manioc, his meager harvests often do not generate enough food for his growing family. His soil lacks nutrients, and he has no fertilizer, good seeds or access to a bank from which to obtain credit to purchase these needed supplies.

He is clearing land for next year's crops. He will use fields he has already cultivated—now depleted of nutrients—for cattle. He has never had legal title to his land and is not sure if he will be able to pass it along to his children. Therefore he must get the most out of it while he lives here.[1]

A fundamental insight of ecology is that everything relates to everything else. Hunger, agriculture, population and the environment are interconnected. The connections can be seen in the United States. The spread of large-scale corporate farming puts pressure on both low-income farmers and the environment, for example, and some populations of low-income people are growing faster than the population at large. But such connections among hunger, population, agriculture and the environment are even more obvious and urgent in developing countries where hunger is prevalent and population growth rapid.

How much environmental damage is caused by poor and hungry people?

Most of the earth's environmental problems are caused by consumption patterns in rich countries. Even in the developing countries, much of the environmental damage is done by relatively affluent people; but the fate of some of the world's threatened ecosystems is also connected to the fate of hungry people. As long as they are desperate for food, fragile ecosystems will be abused and the earth's capacity to feed them will be diminished.

The remaining wild places on earth are typically environments that are difficult for people to exploit. The few people who traditionally inhabited them were extremely poor, sometimes isolated groups such as the Amazon Indians. Today's powerful technologies are bringing dams, commercial logging, oil and mineral exploitation, and agriculture into environments that used to be considered too hostile for these activities. These intrusions threaten the few wild places left on earth and the survival of the people who have lived there for centuries.

In some places, local activists and organizations are working to defend wilderness areas and their traditional inhabitants from commercial development. For example, Chico Menendez gained global fame—and then martyrdom—for organizing people of the Amazon to protect the forest and their livelihoods.

In other places, growing populations of poor people are themselves expanding into fragile ecosystems. At one point during David Beckmann's tenure at the World Bank, he helped the Bank rethink the connection between environment and development. Beckmann visited settlements on the edge of the Amazon and talked with land-hungry settlers like Jose Carvalho. They know that the fragile soils beneath the rain forest can't sustain agriculture for more than a few years, but they don't have another way to make a living.

Beckmann saw how land-starved families were farming steep hillsides in the Philippines. Erosion caused by this farming denudes the mountains and clogs rivers. Flash floods, an increasingly prevalent "natural" disaster in the Philippines, are anything but an act of God.

Beckmann visited Kenyan drylands, where rapid population growth among poor people has led to homesteads where ele-

Connections

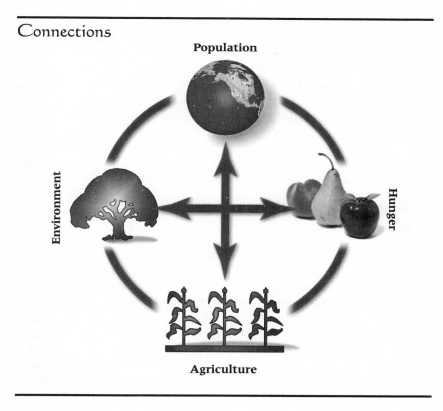

phants and other wildlife used to roam. Farming will turn some of this dryland into desert.

Can't developing countries prevent such damage?

The developing countries are coping with low levels of income, and many people there are willing to put up with some pollution to get better jobs, clothes, food and housing. In fact, it's poverty rather than economic development that causes some of their most pressing environmental problems—such as diseases in drinking water and open sewers in slums. When a family is struggling to survive, foregoing income to protect nature reserves may seem an unaffordable luxury.

Because of the urgent social needs in developing countries, their governments argue that industrial nations should pay most of the cost of action on *global* environmental issues. They persuaded the industrial countries to start a small facility at the World Bank to help underwrite projects that will deal with environmental problems that have worldwide impact. When the International Climate Control Treaty was negotiated in 1998, the developing countries insisted that the industrial nations adopt higher standards for reducing greenhouse gases, because the industrial countries do most of the damage and can better afford pollution control.

Does Bread for the World work with environmental groups?

Environmental and antipoverty groups, such as Bread for the World, often work together to improve international aid programs. While many people think charity is the only way to help hungry people, the environmental movement has always recognized the importance of public policy. The political strength of environmental organizations can make them a good ally in Congress.

Bread for the World's 1993 Offering of Letters, called "Many Neighbors, One Earth," helped develop a sense of common interest between environmental, developmental and religious advocates. The term *sustainable development* had been coined as a name for economic growth coupled with environmental protection. But it has become increasingly clear that sustainable development must include grass-roots participation in decision making and improved livelihoods for poor people—the pattern of development outlined in chapter 6. In 1993, Bread for the World and a diverse array of development and environmental groups urged Congress to make sustainable development, with an emphasis on reducing hunger and poverty, the leading goal of U.S. foreign aid. Congress failed to pass foreign aid reform legislation that would have mandated that policy, but the U.S. Agency for International Development made sustainable development a priority.

Bread for the World's commitment to environmentally sound ways of reducing hunger is grounded in the Bible. The earth is the Lord's, and human beings are its stewards. The Hebrew people had great love for the land, and prophets taught that the land would be fruitful and the nation prosperous only if poor and vulnerable people were treated justly—so closely do justice for hungry people, care of the earth and prosperity intertwine.

Chapter 8

Too Many People?

Why don't poor people quit having so many children? The only solution to the hunger problem is birth control!
—*Letter to Bread for the World*

The world's population has doubled since 1960. It took the entire history of the human race until 1960 to produce a global population of three billion, but only half a lifetime for global population to reach six billion in 1999. The United Nations projects that by the year 2050, there will be between 7.3 billion and 10.7 billion people on the planet, but the projection it calls most likely is 8.9 billion.[1] Where the actual size of the human population will fall within this wide range depends a lot on the action or inaction of the world's nations in the next few years.

What are the consequences of rapid population growth?

One consequence is environmental stress. Most environmental stress can be traced to consumption in industrial nations, but developing countries are straining their own fragile ecosystems through increasing numbers of people and rising standards of living. This undercuts their ability to lift themselves out of poverty and sustain a growing population. With too few resources to meet existing needs, they face expanding demands for schools, jobs, water systems and much more. Where population growth strains land and water resources, agricultural productivity and farm incomes drop, and competition for land and water can even lead to conflict.

At the family level, poor couples tend to have more children than others, even when they can't provide adequately for the children. With each new child often comes:

World Population Growth—
The current era of world population growth is unprecedented
(Population growth in developed and developing countries 1750–1990; years 2000–2050 estimated)

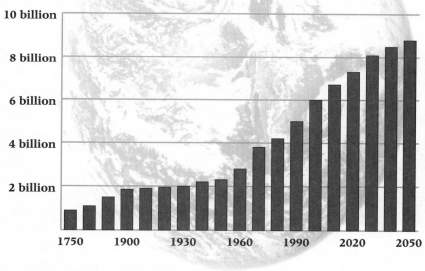

Source: United Nations Population Division,
World Population Prospects: The 1998 revision, forthcoming.

- less attention and fewer resources for each child
- less time for the mother to earn income
- more crowding
- less food for the family

Why, then, do poor people have so many children?

There are many reasons. Children bring love and satisfaction to parents everywhere, and impoverished parents may have few other satisfactions. Most cultures traditionally celebrate big families. For many parents, the harshness of poverty and lack of education make planning ahead difficult. Many couples believe that contraception is sinful or have no access to family planning services. More children add labor and therefore may add food and income to a farm family.

One major motive is that poor parents in developing countries need surviving sons to provide for them in old age. Surviving sons are their social security. But an African child is 20 times more likely to die before the age of five than a child born in the United States. Under such conditions, making sure you have surviving sons means having many children. Because good nutrition and health care give parents assurance that their children will survive, they are key factors in reducing population growth, just as slowing population growth is important for the reduction of hunger.

What other factors are important in slowing population growth?

As a rule, when poor people have opportunities to increase their incomes and see hope for a better future, they are more likely to limit the size of their families. Improving the lives of poor women may be the single most effective way to curtail population growth *and* reduce hunger. Women who can read tend to have fewer children. Women who share in family decision making usually allow more space between pregnancies and experience better health. As they become educated and economically empowered, women are better able to prevent their children from becoming malnourished and succumbing to deadly childhood diseases. Knowing that their children are more likely to survive and thrive, they feel less pressure to have more children.

In short, reducing hunger and poverty, especially among women and small children, reduces population growth. The availability of family planning services has also been an important factor in the reduction of population growth. Urbanization plays a part as well, because families that live in the city are more crowded and more often prompted by financial considerations toward fewer children.

What caused the world's population to soar suddenly in the twentieth century?

Not higher birth rates, but lower death rates. Advances in medicine and public health, along with increases in food production, have enabled people to live longer. And as more people survive to adulthood, they have more children.

The population explosion actually began in Europe and the United States. In 1800 about 22 percent of the human race was Caucasian; but by 1930 (only six generations later) that percentage had jumped to about 35. This happened because new technologies pushed back the death rate among white European peoples. Industrial growth and the colonization of new lands (including most of the United States) absorbed this growing population. Then, as living standards rose, the birth and population growth rates began to recede.

Public health measures, which developed slowly in the West, were made available more rapidly in the developing countries, so their populations soared suddenly. Poor countries can thank the West for medical advances—and for the population explosion.

Is the population explosion completely out of control?

Happily, the rate of world population growth has decreased by more than a third, from its annual peak of 2.04 percent during the 1965–1970 period to 1.33 percent during 1995–2000; and it will fall to 0.34 percent by midcentury, according to U.N. projections. World population growth peaked at 86 million annually during the 1985–1990 period, and fell to an annual average of less than 78 million during 1995–2000.[2]

Even more striking, the number of children per woman of childbearing age in developing countries fell over the past 30 years from an average of six to three.[3] That's a dramatic drop. But it takes time for lower birth rates to slow the population growth rate, because a high birth rate leads to a second wave of births when the first generation reaches childbearing age, and because people are living longer.

Doesn't the Roman Catholic Church oppose efforts to curb population growth?

The Vatican acknowledges the need to reduce rapid population growth. But it places this concern within the context of its teachings about the dignity of all people, the need for equitable and sustainable development, and respect for a married couple's desire to decide voluntarily on the number and spacing of children.

The positions of both population control advocates and their religious opponents have evolved over the decades. In the 1960s and 1970s, some population control advocates acted as if *the* solution to the population explosion was the dissemination of contraceptives. The Catholic Church was opposed to artificial contraception and argued that the real challenge was to support development in poor countries and fully welcome newly born children to the banquet of life.

The world's experience since then has confirmed that progress against hunger and poverty curbs population growth. Population groups now try to integrate their work with general efforts to improve health, educate girls and foster development. On the other hand, the Vatican clearly sees the need to curb population growth. The Catholic Church opposes coercive methods of population control as well as abortion and artificial methods of birth control. It insists that family planning programs should respect individual consciences and religious beliefs, but it also encourages natural family planning and access to health services for women. In Kenya, which is struggling with one of the highest population growth rates in the world, the Catholic Church is part of the national population council.

Because Bread for the World works with the Roman Catholic Church and a diverse array of Protestant churches, whose positions on birth control vary, it seeks common ground with these churches while stressing that the curtailing of rapid population growth is a necessary part of overcoming hunger.

What about consumption levels among the world's better-off people? If that causes more environmental stress than population growth among poor people, what can be done about it?

Some forms of affluence—the enjoyment of a painting, for example, or improvements in computer technology—do virtually no harm to the environment. But burning up fossil fuels does irreversible damage. Air and water pollution effects are often irreversible as well.

Individuals can, as a matter of conscience, reduce their own consumption of non-renewable resources. More powerfully, laws can regulate and tax the use of such resources. Such laws in the world's rich countries are the logical counterpart to efforts in the developing countries to reduce population growth.

Another negative impact of excessive consumption among the world's well-off people—which includes the authors and most of the readers of this book—is a misdirection of energy. Affluent people tend to keep themselves excessively busy and spend enormous amounts of money on frivolous, ultimately unsatisfying, material consumption. Simpler living can free money and precious time for family, God and people in need.

Lowering consumption in itself does nothing to bring impoverished people to the table. For that to happen, a transfer must be arranged. Eating bread instead of beef or not buying a new car helps hungry people only if the person foregoing those purchases contributes the amount saved to someone in need or to an assistance or advocacy group. On a much larger scale, rich nations could increase assistance to poor countries for things like agricultural research and self-help opportunities, and invest more in efforts to reduce hunger in their own countries. Reallocating resources on the scale needed to eliminate most hunger would not even require less consumption by affluent people, but merely a modest drop in the rate at which consumption increases.

Chapter 9
Too Little Food?

Journalist T. R. Reid was interviewing Ho Zhiqian, a nutrition expert and professor at Sun Yat-sen Medical University:

> "Can the earth continue to feed its growing population?" he asked. "Oh, Mr. Reid, you've asked the wrong person," he replied. "I've devoted my life to the study of food supplies, diet, and nutrition. But your question goes way beyond those fields. Can the earth feed all its people? That, I'm afraid, is strictly a political question."[1]

Twenty-five years ago, in 1974, some experts were alarmed that world food production might not keep pace with population growth. Environmentalist Paul Ehrlich warned of massive famines and said that feeding six million people "is totally impossible."[2] Instead, thanks in large part to the green revolution, food production has surpassed population growth.

But the green revolution bypassed many of the poorest farmers, and agriculture today places a tremendous strain on the earth's land and water resources. Partly because of land and environmental limits, grain production (which provides more than 80 percent of the world's food) has lagged slightly behind population since 1984. What's needed now is another green revolution, one that Gordon Conway, ecologist and agricultural researcher who heads the Rockefeller Foundation, calls a "doubly green revolution" because it has to do two things: boost the productivity of poor farmers who can't afford costly technologies and sustain the environment.[3] Without such a revolution, feeding the world's people and protecting the earth's land and water resources will be next to impossible.

What's the story of the green revolution?

One day in 1963, in row 288 on a field of the International Rice Research Institute (IRRI) in the Philippines, Dr. Henry Beachell, an agronomist, spotted an unusual stalk of rice. It was uncommonly short and sturdy, and in it he saw the potential for a new kind of rice that would hold fertilizer well, resist pest damage and yield more than conventional strains. Beachell called this rice IR-8, because it was the research station's eighth cross between rice varieties.

When IR-8 was released to the public three years later, it changed the face of world agriculture. It is now planted in 70 percent of the world's rice fields and has doubled worldwide rice production.[4] Most U.S.-grown rice comes from IRRI strains—an example of what we learn from developing countries, and the payoff for assisting them.

Equally dramatic gains were achieved in wheat production. Norman Borlaug, an Iowa farmer turned agronomist, received a Nobel Peace Prize for his research on high-yield strains of dwarf wheat. India and Pakistan were on the brink of widespread famine in the mid-1960s, before dwarf wheat yielded enough grain to feed their growing populations. When Borlaug arrived

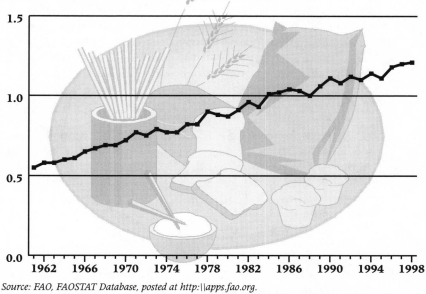

World Grain Yield Per Acre, 1961–1998 *(in tons)*

Source: FAO, FAOSTAT Database, posted at http://apps.fao.org.

in the region, Pakistan was harvesting about three million tons of wheat per year and India 11 million. Today Pakistan harvests around 18 million tons of wheat per year and India 60 million.

These production gains, which also include corn, came to be called the green revolution in agriculture. But the fertilizers, pesticides and irrigation required to implement that revolution led to environmental problems. Also, more prosperous farmers owned land and could afford fertilizers, pesticides and irrigation pumps, so they seized an opportunity that impoverished farmers often could not. However, poor families in both rural and urban areas benefited from lower food prices, and some of the rural poor from job opportunities. Overall, the green revolution made a great contribution, both in food and jobs, to the struggle against hunger.

But is there enough food to feed the world?

The world now produces enough food for every person to consume 2,720 calories per day, on average. That is well over what is considered the minimum daily requirement of 2,350.[5] The problem, right now, is primarily one of distribution. The main way food gets distributed is by being sold and bought on the free market, so families need enough income to purchase food or they will go hungry. For this reason hunger often exists right alongside of food surpluses, as it does in the United States, while Japan, which imports most of its food, has little incidence of hunger.

Does U.S. agriculture contribute to overcoming hunger?

U.S. agriculture has long led the world in using technology and raising productivity. U.S. farmers help to feed much of the world. About half of the world's grain exports come from the United States. In 1997 the United States exported $57 billion worth of agricultural products.[6]

Important and growing exports to the Middle East and East Asia have shown the U.S. agricultural community that it has a self-interest stake in overcoming world hunger. When hungry people begin to raise their standard of living, a large share of their increased spending goes for food. They diversify their diets, and that may include some imported food.

U.S. food aid plays a vital role in humanitarian emergencies worldwide and has provided a supplement to U.S. financial aid to poor countries. But food aid is tiny in relation to the scale of world hunger. As international trade agreements and U.S. laws have reduced subsidies to U.S. and European farmers, global food aid has declined, from 16.8 million metric tons in 1993 to 6.6 million tons in 1997.[7] Also, food aid is not a substitute for improving local agriculture. Food aid must be carefully targeted (for school children, for example, or in exchange for work on development projects) so that it doesn't undercut local farmers.

The efficiency of U.S. agriculture has helped reduce hunger in the United States by keeping food prices low. That's important to poor families, who spend a higher proportion of their income on food than better-off families.

But an underside to U.S. agriculture is rural poverty. The changing structure of U.S. agriculture has contributed to rural poverty. About 4 percent of U.S. farms now account for over half of gross sales, leaving many small farms with little production and narrow profits.[8] Droves of farmers have been forced to sell out, and most families on small farms depend partly on jobs in town to make a living.

U.S. agriculture is also straining the nation's natural resources. Fertilizers and pesticides add to water pollution, and ground and surface water supplies have been reduced.

The United States needs to be part of the doubly green revolution, coupling its continuing drive for productivity with care for the environment and measures to reduce rural poverty.

What are the environmental constraints on global agriculture?

One big constraint is that the world is running out of unused farmland. Part of the agricultural growth of the last generation came from bringing more land under cultivation. But only 10 percent of the earth's land can be cultivated,[9] and about 95 percent of all tillable soil is now being farmed. According to Norman Borlaug, only parts of Africa, the Cerrado region of Brazil and some of the former Soviet Republics have significant amounts of arable land that can be developed.[10]

Population growth, urbanization, overcultivation and unsustainable agricultural practices are degrading large tracts of land. Farms get swallowed up to make room for houses, roads and industries. Overgrazing or the slashing and burning of forests has rendered other land useless. Chemicals and irrigation without proper drainage have added to the damage. Twenty percent of the earth's land surface has been degraded to some extent.[11]

So will food supplies fall short?

It depends on whom you ask. Lester Brown, president of Worldwatch Institute, is pessimistic about the impact of environmental factors on food production. He predicts large-scale food shortages in the not-too-distant future. Yield increases for some crops have been leveling off, and Brown thinks that agriculture is running up against biological limits.[12]

The U.N. Food and Agriculture Organization (FAO), on the other hand, expects food production to outpace population growth. While Brown interprets the slowdown in growth of crop yields as global ecosystem fatigue, FAO notes that there are also other reasons—such as reduced promotion of agricultural development and the fact that many people are satisfied with their current levels of consumption.[13] Bread for the World leans toward the FAO analysis, but no one can be sure.

Are we running out of water, too?

The lack of usable water is a serious constraint and will become far more serious. One-third of the world's food is harvested from irrigated land, and 70 percent of the water drawn from rivers or underground sources is used for irrigation. Population and economic growth increase demand for fresh water. But the per capita supply has been declining for two decades, as underground water tables fall and many rivers are gradually being drained. This decline is partly responsible for the slow growth in the world's grain harvest since 1984. Lester Brown says that "spreading water scarcity may be the most underrated resource issue in the world today."[14]

More and more, industrial and urban needs compete with agriculture for water. In this competition, numbers of people and political pressures often favor urban needs. As for the economic side, it takes a thousand tons of water to produce $200 worth of wheat *or* to increase industrial output by $14,000, a 70 to 1 advantage for industry.[15] For example, China may be forced to greatly increase grain imports—partly because its expanding population and industrial growth are encroaching on cropland— but partly to divert more water for industrial and urban uses. That would place further demand on food production elsewhere and could drive prices up.[16]

Water problems cause hunger in other ways as well. The polluting of waters, along with overfishing, has contributed to a near leveling (and per capita decline) in the global fish catch since 1988. More than a billion people in developing countries have no access to clean water; the result is diseases that waste both nutrition and lives. And in the future, competition for water may trigger more wars than competition for land—violence that would certainly contribute to hunger.

How can we cope with water shortages?

There are two main solutions. The one with the most immediate impact is more efficient use of water. That speaks to personal choices people make, but much more to policies that often subsidize the wasteful use of water. The solution with the greatest potential long-term impact is desalination. The oceans account for more than 97 percent of the earth's water, but desalination is still a fledgling technology, too expensive in most places to compete with other sources, but slowly becoming more competitive. Presidents Eisenhower and Kennedy vigorously supported desalination efforts and for a while the United States led the world in desalination research, spending $144 million (adjusted for inflation) in 1977. In 1982, federal support was largely abandoned and eventually shriveled to less than two million dollars.[17]

Water conservation, desalination research and the provision of drinkable water to poor communities all require government policy initiatives. In 1995 Ismail Serageldin, a vice president for the World Bank, announced: "We are warning the world that there is a huge problem looming out there. . . . The experts all agree on need to do something fast. The main problem is the lack of political will. . . ."[18]

What else can be done to increase food production?

Investment in agriculture and agricultural research must increase, with research focused on agricultural improvements that are environmentally sustainable and that small-scale farmers can use. While genetic engineering poses serious environmental and ethical risks, it can, if wisely deployed, help the world feed its growing population. An even bigger challenge for researchers may be listening to poor farmers and building on traditional wisdom. That's not the way scientists usually do business.

The international network of agricultural research institutes that made the green revolution possible are now leading work on the "doubly green revolution." They need more funding. But the nations of the world sharply reduced funding for agriculture and agricultural research in the 1980s. Happily, it is now increasing again.

World grain reserves are another uncertainty. In 1997, world grain stocks held only enough to support 56 days of consumption, one of the lowest numbers on record. Supplies subsequently increased, but if widespread shortages were to occur under such conditions, prices would soar and vast numbers of poor people would go hungry.

What is Bread for the World doing to help make sure that the world has enough food?

Bread for the World's 1998 Offering of Letters, called *Africa: Seeds of Hope*, pushed for increased U.S. aid and private investment in African agriculture and rural development. The *Africa: Seeds of Hope* bill, drafted with the assistance of Bread for the World, also directed the U.S. Agency for International Development (USAID) to provide leadership in improving agricultural research. In addition, the bill established a routine mechanism to replenish the U.S. grain reserve for use in humanitarian emergencies.

Bread for the World members across the country won political support—one senator and one representative at a time. The efforts of Bread members in Cincinnati, Ohio, illustrate what it takes. When Steve Chabot, a conservative Republican, was first elected to Congress in 1995, he was assigned to the Africa

Subcommittee of the International Relations Committee. The local Bread for the World group began meeting with Chabot shortly after he took office. Chabot, a Catholic, and Mike Gable, a pastoral associate at a Catholic parish, brought priests who worked in Africa to talk with Chabot. This education and relationship building paid off. In June 1995, Chabot pushed through an amendment to increase development funding for Africa by $20 million.

"As soon as we learned he was going to be assigned to the Africa subcommittee, we asked him to visit Africa," says Gable. "He finally told us he would go to Africa if he won reelection. After he won the election, we went back to him and asked him, 'When are you going?' We kept the pressure on every time we saw him." Chabot made the trip to Africa in August 1997.

Then came Bread for the World's Offering of Letters, *Africa: Seeds of Hope*. Parishioners from seven churches in the Cincinnati area wrote about 200 letters asking Chabot and other local members of Congress to cosponsor the *Africa: Seeds of Hope* Act. Bread for the World members followed up with phone calls to Chabot's Washington office. Bread for the World activists Bob Ehrsam and Sister Mary Cabrini Durkin convinced the *Cincinnati Enquirer* to publish an editorial endorsing the legislation.

Finally, these local Bread leaders organized a picnic and invited the aides affiliated with local members of Congress to attend. They asked them publicly if they would support the bill. Chabot's aide announced that Chabot would cosponsor the *Africa: Seeds of Hope* Act.

One week later, on June 22, the bill came up for a vote in the House International Relations Committee. Chabot spoke eloquently in support of the legislation. The committee voted unanimously to approve the legislation. David Beckmann was there to thank Chabot, and he replied, "You certainly have active people in Cincinnati."

The *Africa: Seeds of Hope* Act passed Congress and became law in November 1998. Bread for the World Institute will monitor its implications, working together with grassroots groups in Africa.

Increased U.S. aid for African agriculture will be good news for people like Phillipa Louse of Munhacua in Mozambique. This village was completely destroyed by rebel attacks during a brutal civil war. The villagers' land was rendered useless. In 1986, the private aid agency, World Vision, with help from USAID, began supplying Mozambique with agricultural kits, tools and training. Despite the difficult nature of restoring normalcy to this war-devastated place—"This is more than I bargained for," said World Vision agronomist Mauro Netto at the time—it paid off. After four years of agricultural assistance, Phillipa Louse's *machamba*, or farm, produces cassava, rice, sweet potatoes, maize and sugar cane.[19]

Some Bread for the World members in Cincinnati contribute to World Vision, Catholic Relief Services, Church World Service or other agencies that do similar work in Africa. But those members helped African farmers on a far larger scale by influencing their representative in Congress. Both types of responses are essential, and in combination they spread a bigger table for everyone.

A
Jobs-Based
Strategy

Chapter 10

Creating Good Jobs

> When Oxfam was distributing food rations in Cambodia dur-
> ing the famine, hundreds of people waited quietly for their
> share. But when fish nets were handed out, the crowd
> cheered. —*Joe Short*[1]

When hungry people are asked what they need most, they typically say a job or a better paying job. Poor people in the United
States would nearly all rather have a decent job than rely on
public assistance. Hungry farmers in India want land, ways of
getting more production from their land and better prices for the
crops they sell, because the land is their livelihood.

As global population grows, the labor force will grow at an
even faster rate, from 2.7 billion to more than four billion workers. If part of the billion-plus workers presently unemployed or
underemployed are added, more than two billion new economic
opportunities are needed by 2025.[2]

How can enough jobs be found for a growing world population already struggling to feed itself?

Jobs aren't going to be *found* anywhere. People have to generate
productive work opportunities, and that task will fall largely to
the private sector. Businesses can expand to meet the needs and
aspirations of a growing population. Entrepreneurs and business
managers play a crucial role in organizing production and
employment opportunities. In addition, many low-income people
organize little businesses of their own.

Government needs to encourage a favorable environment
for private-sector development by avoiding unnecessary taxes
and regulations and by managing its own budget and the money
supply carefully. Government agencies also do a great range of
other things that are essential to a healthy economy—from

building highways to enforcing regulations regarding food, transportation and workplace safety. Governments can also ensure that everyone has access to the education and health care they need to be productive, and that there is a safety net for people who cannot support themselves.

What can be done to make sure that workers get paid a livable wage?

This is an urgent question in the United States, where declining wages have been a major cause of growing hunger.

The Earned Income Tax Credit (EITC) is one of the best mechanisms the U.S. government has to make sure that workers earn enough to feed their families. Progressive income tax, requiring a higher rate of payment for those with higher incomes, puts a heavier tax burden on those who can better afford it. During the Reagan administration, the principle was extended in the other direction by expanding the EITC. Workers whose households fall below specified wage levels receive a reimbursement on taxes paid or in some cases even a subsidy. The lower the income, the greater the subsidy. Many conservatives prefer EITC to increases in the minimum wage, because EITC distorts market incentives less.

The minimum wage is important. In the late 1960s a full-time job at the minimum wage kept a family of three out of poverty. But in 1997 the minimum wage was $5.15 an hour, while it took $7.90 an hour, or $16,400 a year (plus health insurance), to bring a family of four above the poverty line. Various combinations of minimum-wage and EITC increases could assure all workers a livable wage. The important thing is to reward work and make work pay.

The government also plays a role in assuring the right of workers to form unions and bargain collectively. Unions enjoy less public sympathy than they once did, but they help to raise wages (at least for specific groups of workers), protect workers from arbitrary and abusive treatment and support government policies that are in the interest of workers.

The government can serve as the employer of last resort. There are plenty of things that need to be done to contribute to the quality of life in our communities, and it is much better—

better for them, better for all of us—to have people work as public employees than to be thrown into destitution or become welfare recipients.

Public investments in health, education and nutrition help people become productive, well-paid workers.

Finally, there are safety net programs. Some people cannot and should not work—elderly and disabled people, for example, or people with family members who require full-time care. As long as government policies don't assure a job with a livable wage for everyone who can work, unemployed people and low-wage workers will also require help to meet their basic needs.

What about jobs in developing countries?

Ninety-five percent of the two billion new jobs needed by 2025 will be in developing countries.[3] The needs are vast, and the capacities of developing-country governments are limited. So even more so than in richer countries, private sector enterprise must carry the bulk of the load.

Developing-country governments can also make sure that everyone has access to basic health and nutrition and protect basic labor rights. But schemes like the Earned Income Tax Credit are beyond what most governments can afford or effectively implement. Some developing countries have written lots of economic regulations and high taxes into the law, but don't effectively enforce the law. As a result, businesses and higher-income people often devote energy to evading laws rather than to obeying them. Better to have fewer regulations and focus on enforcing them.

A large percentage of the poorest people in developing countries depend heavily on farming for their livelihood, so improvements in agriculture can lift many farm families out of poverty. But with little new land to open for cultivation, farming will be able to absorb relatively few additional workers. Some of the sons and daughters of farmers can develop off-farm jobs in rural areas. Others will add to the rapid expansion of cities, where a growing share of the world's hungry people live.

City dwellers lose much of the social safety net that extended families in rural areas provide. New immigrants to urban areas have to spend months or years looking for jobs. But city jobs typically pay enough, compared to the levels of income in rural areas, to make the wait worthwhile. Urban slums are crowded and unsanitary, but they often offer schools, clinics and other amenities that are less available in rural areas. One of the authors (Beckmann) worked five years on slum improvement programs in Latin America and Africa, and learned to appreciate the dynamism of many poor people in the burgeoning cities of developing countries.

Most of the world's poorest people never have wage-paying jobs. They are self-employed and often garner their livelihoods from various sources. A poor family in a Latin American city may include one person who works in a business and earns a wage and another adult who runs a small business from their home; the older children will help with the home-based business or find after-school jobs in the neighborhood. A poor woman in rural Africa may have a small plot of land that she cultivates for food, but she will do other things to eke out a tenuous existence for her family: produce handicrafts for sale, perform odd jobs for a better-off neighbor and gather wood from the land around her village to make charcoal.

Will microenterprise programs help?

Microenterprise credit is a promising, relatively new approach to job creation among low-income groups. The Grameen Bank (the "rural bank") in Bangladesh developed techniques that have allowed it to lend money to more than a million tiny enterprises—to impoverished widows, for example, to buy and sell chickens or sew for their neighbors. Commercial banks wouldn't lend to poor people because they were considered bad credit risks. But the Grameen Bank and similar organizations in other parts of the developing world found that they could lend to small *groups* of very low-income people. Repayment rates are typically 90 to 95 percent.

The Foundation for International Community Assistance (FINCA) runs microenterprise programs in a number of countries, including Uganda. Tibiwa Asani was a founding member of FINCA's village bank in Bugembe, a village in Uganda. Her husband is a janitor/watchman in a feed store, and his income isn't enough to feed their family. Tibiwa tried to contribute income by opening a little grocery stand, but the stand was poorly stocked and produced little revenue.

The village bank provides loans of $50 to $100 dollars to women building their own businesses. In groups of 20 to 40 women, clients approve and guarantee each other's loans, establish and manage a collective savings account, keep their own books, enforce repayment and learn to run a democratic organization. The repayment rate for FINCA Uganda loans is nearly 100 percent.

With her first loan of $75, Tibiwa purchased 50 broiler chickens. She purchased feed on credit from the store where her husband works and used the profits from her grocery stand to meet her weekly payments of capital, interest and savings to the village bank.

Today Tibiwa is raising 600 birds. She can sell a chicken for about three or four dollars. Her daily profits are now around $16, and she has been able to accumulate an amazing $600 in savings. In addition, Tibiwa has put all six of her school-age children in boarding school. She purchased a cow that provides milk to her family. With the poultry and eggs in their diet, malnutrition no longer endangers the members of Tibiwa's family.[4]

Results, an antihunger advocacy group with which Bread for the World often works, has managed to get many grass-roots groups, governments and international agencies to commit themselves to a dramatic expansion of microenterprise credit programs such as FINCA Uganda. Some organizations have already demonstrated that this approach can work in the United States, too. Microenterprise credit is a promising targeted approach, like child survival programs. If its ongoing expansion is handled well, it could help millions of poor people increase their income.

Maria Otero, formerly chair of Bread for the World's board, is executive vice president of ACCION, which promotes microenterprise development in the Americas. She has prompted microcredit agencies, banks and government officials to think about how to open the regular banking system to small-scale entrepreneurs.

Some microenterprise agencies have turned themselves into commerical banks, and are thus able to do business with poor people on a much larger scale. ACCION International has managed to attract capital from the financial markets of the world and channel it into tiny loans to microbusinesses. It is also working with governments to help change laws and regulations that discourage banks from lending to poor people.

The nonprofit agency that ACCION developed in Bolivia has become a successful and expanding bank, called Banco Sol. Some other banks in Bolivia have noted that Banco Sol's innovations are profitable, and they are now competing with Banco Sol to provide loans and other banking services to Bolivia's poor majority. This would have been unthinkable 15 years ago.

Aren't many people poor because their culture is not conducive to work and success?

The values and aspirations of most poor people in the United States largely coincide with those of the population as a whole. And many poor families, despite daunting obstacles, manage to overcome or enable their children to overcome poverty. Coauthor Arthur Simon lived for 21 years in a poverty-stricken neighborhood in New York. The vast majority of people there *did* work, and most unemployed people *wanted* to work. However, many were handicapped by limited skills, poor education or emotional or physical disorders. Some were on drugs or engaged in criminal behavior. For some the welfare syndrome and the cycle of poverty carried over from one generation to another and discouraged a work ethic. Out-of-wedlock births were common. So the need for a sense of hope, improved habits, skills, moral standards and more parental involvement in the education of children presents a huge challenge, one in which the churches could play a much larger role.

Coauthor Beckmann has worked in a number of developing countries. Some cultures encourage work and efficiency more than others, but the great majority of people in developing countries are striving to raise their standard of living. That often includes wrenching changes in culture. In Beckmann's experience, poor people in developing countries generally work incredibly hard to stave off hunger. But hard work and willingness to work will have to be combined with private and public efforts on an unprecedented scale in order to give the future labor force a place at the table.

Chapter 11
Investing in People

When I was superintendent of a large school system, I saw
children who fell asleep at their desks. One child, when asked
if he had eaten any breakfast, replied, "It wasn't my turn."
—*Christine Vladimiroff, O.S.B.*[1]

Hunger can and often does cause permanent setbacks in brain
development, but, as the child above reminds us, it can also just
make learning difficult. In a small way the child illustrates the
connection between health and education as well as the connection of both to hunger and poverty.

Hungry people tend to have much poorer health than those
who are well fed, and poor health may cause frequent absence
from school as well as learning difficulties in school. In developing countries, for families too poor to afford enough to eat,
paying even modest school fees is often beyond reach. But a long
walk to school may be physically too demanding for weakened
children, so many do not attend.

That indicates how hunger may affect health and education, but how do health and education affect hunger?

Poor health care and little education hinder the ability of people
to increase their earnings and provide adequately for their families. Not surprisingly, statistics show a high correlation between
inadequate health care and education on the one hand, and
poverty and hunger on the other.

Can it be shown, then, that improvements in health and education lead to a reduction of hunger?

That's clear regarding countless individuals but also apparent
from global statistics. Developing countries have registered

dramatic improvements in the rates of infant mortality, life expectancy, literacy and school attendance. But the gains are uneven from country to country. Where they are the highest, hunger and poverty have been greatly reduced. And where the gains are quite limited, countries have made little or no progress against hunger.

As chapter 3 noted, some of the East Asian countries made dramatic and sustained headway against hunger and poverty. Why? Shortly after World War II, nations such as China, South Korea and Taiwan extended education and health care to everyone. They invested in their people. At the time they were very poor countries. In no small part because of health and education, these countries not only spread the benefits of development more evenly among their people than most other countries did, but their economies also grew more rapidly.

What type of health care and education makes the biggest difference?

World Bank analysis has shown that primary education and primary health care yield the highest returns, even by strictly economic calculations. Neighborhood clinics and village health practitioners do more to improve health than expensive hospitals; a dollar for preventive care does more than a dollar invested in curative medicine. Nutrition, sanitation, safe drinking water and basic medicines for the most common ailments are also inexpensive measures that make a big difference and can lift the health of the entire population. In education, elementary schools should take priority over secondary schools and colleges.

Health and education for infants and young children, and for girls generally, have especially high payoffs in terms of both human welfare and national development. The HIV/AIDS epidemic also demands special attention.

AIDS is a threat to life, but how is it a threat to poverty reduction?

HIV/AIDS typically kills young adults who have just entered the most productive years of life and are often best positioned to move families and communities forward. Instead, they are leaving behind orphaned children. Relatives, sometimes aged grand-parents, have to take them in, but often cannot afford to feed additional children or send them to school. In 1997, almost one-fourth of Zambia's children under fifteen had lost one or both parents, and almost three-fourths of all households were taking care of at least one orphan. In addition, 90 thousand children were living on the street in Lusaka, the capital city.[2]

Africa accounts for 91 percent of all AIDS deaths. Of 30 million people infected by HIV worldwide as of 1998, 26 million live in 34 African countries. In some of those countries more than 20 percent of the adult population is infected. In Botswana, life expectancy during a recent five-year period dropped from 61 to 47 years and was expected to fall to 41 before the year 2005.[3]

The loss in terms of human suffering, livelihoods, incomes, nutrition, production and community leadership is enormous. Most people and communities are coping through the extended family system, though this is being strained beyond capacity at times. HIV/AIDS adds one more obstacle to the struggle against hunger and poverty. It illustrates the key role that health—like that of education—plays in successful development.

Are there lessons for the United States in these experiences of developing countries?

The basic lesson is that investing in people is not only morally right but smart. Healthy and well-educated or well-trained people become productive assets to any country, and unhealthy people or those poorly equipped to create or find good jobs often become a drain. The United States can invest on the front end to make sure its people have access to adequate health care and education, or it can pay on the back end in lost productivity, hunger, poverty and social problems.

Regarding health care, almost all other industrial nations offer coverage for everyone. But the United States had 43 million people (16 percent of the population) without health insurance coverage for the entire 1997 calendar year, according to the Census Bureau, and those numbers were rising. They included almost 11 million children, nearly one-third of all poor people and one-half of the working poor. That puts a large segment of the population an illness or an accident away from financial disaster. It has forced many people to forego needed medical treatment, choose between medical care and food, or quit work.

The picture on education is more complicated. The United States has a public education system that enables, even compels, everyone to go to school. Its postsecondary education system is the envy of the world. Excellence is less clear at the elementary and secondary levels. Schools in low-income neighborhoods often lack adequate staffing, textbooks and supplies, and building maintenance. Many serve a disproportionate share of children with social handicaps, some prone to violence. The nation's richest school districts spend 56 percent more per student than do the poorest because the funding base (property taxes) favors wealthier neighborhoods.[4] Relative to other professions, teachers' salaries are low, and gifted students who might prefer to teach sometimes choose not to, or move to other professions after a discouraging year or two in an inner-city school.

But aren't parents often the ones who fail rather than schools or teachers?

Many parents, often just one parent, and a higher proportion of low-income parents, do not spend time with their children's education. They may not know that conversing a lot with infants and toddlers and reading to them stimulate early brain development. When their children start school, they may assume that education is the teacher's job. Low-income parents especially are often swamped with other problems. Yet parental involvement is the single most important factor in a child's learning. So parental leadership needs to be combined with school improvements.

And what is the importance of this concerning hunger?

Everywhere in the world education and training are keys for escaping the poverty that spawns hunger. In the United States the wages of low-skilled workers have declined mainly because of the growing importance of knowledge in the information economy. International competition has also been a factor. Poorly educated U.S. workers now compete directly with workers in Mexico and Indonesia, for example. The best way to counteract both of these pressures is to invest more in education, health and nutrition for everyone in the United States.

Can nutrition programs really be considered an investment?

Yes, and that's most clearly the case for child nutrition programs. Hungry children have a hard time concentrating, are more likely to have headaches and to miss school because of illness. "Inadequate nutrition . . . is [directly] associated with increased educational failure among impoverished children."[5] Children who do not get a decent education are far less likely than others to be able to support a family as adults. So investing in child nutrition and education is part of a jobs-based approach to overcoming hunger.

Rachel Jones, a reporter for the Knight-Ridder newspapers, reflects on her own childhood in Cairo, Illinois:

> [H]unger is a very real barrier to learning. I know what it's like to sit at a school desk with no little brown paper sack from home, having not eaten breakfast and with no quarters for lunch. A hot breakfast or a nourishing lunch can make all the difference to a poor child. A full stomach is a terrific equalizer. It gave me one less thing to worry about and provided me with the fuel to keep studying and keep expanding my mind.[6]

The school lunch program is the best-known child nutrition program, but the less utilized school breakfast program provides free or reduced-price breakfasts to low-income children. Low-income children who receive school breakfasts score significantly higher on standardized tests and tend to be absent or tardy less often than low-income children who do not benefit from the school breakfast program.

Many school districts pass up the federal funding that is available for school breakfasts, sometimes just because they don't want to bother with a school breakfast program. Concerned citizens can insist that their local schools make breakfast available.

The WIC program, described in chapter 5, assures proper

nutrition during crucial periods of pregnancy, infancy and early childhood.

The food stamp program is by far the biggest child nutrition program. Sixty percent of the recipients of food stamps are families with children.[7] But the food stamp program currently provides only about seventy-five cents per person per meal. Much of the hunger suffered in the United States comes toward the end of each month when food stamps run out.

Cathy Brechtelsbauer, volunteer coordinator for Bread for the World in South Dakota, wrote about families there who find that each month is about one week too long:

> One mother I know pours water on her child's cereal. It doesn't happen every day, only after the food stamps run out for the month. It breaks her heart, because she is nutrition conscious and studying to become a nurse. She is intelligent and manages the best she can under her circumstances.

National nutrition programs—school meals, WIC and food stamps—are a remarkably efficient and effective way of reducing hunger. Their main weakness is underfunding. Simply expanding these nutrition programs could quickly end most hunger in the United States. This investment in nutrition for all would also help the whole population be more productive and contribute to a durable, job-based approach to ending U.S. hunger.

Chapter 12

Welfare Reform

April Rupe was a welfare mother until she started working at a nursing home. Now she can pay her bills, but doing so requires occasional 12- and 18-hour shifts and sometimes work on days off. "It's hard when you've got a four-year-old and he's saying, 'Mommy, stay home,'" she says.

One thing hasn't changed. This family was poor when they were on welfare, and they are poor now. Although Athens County, Ohio, has cut half of the families, like Ms. Rupe's, off the welfare rolls, its poverty rate stubbornly remains at more than 30 percent.

Is this, as some say, a sign of success—a sign that the habit of dependency is being broken and the work ethic instilled? Or, as others say, does it show that that much more needs to be done?[1]

The United States is engaged in a major controversial experiment in social policy: welfare reform. Bread for the World favors welfare reform but opposed the bill that went before Congress in 1996. Bread for the World fought, with success, to maintain food stamps as a federal program. However, Congress approved other changes by a large margin, and President Clinton signed them into law.

Welfare reform is probably the main reason why the strong economy in the late 1990s has not reduced hunger. But welfare reform also includes some promising new approaches. As midcourse corrections of welfare reform are done, the nation should build on approaches that work and correct the mistakes.

Doesn't welfare reform represent the kind of jobs-centered approach to reducing poverty and hunger that Bread for the World advocates?

The 1996 welfare reform law was based on three ideas: first, that poor people should work; second, that state or local governments

87

should administer welfare; and third, that funding for welfare and other social programs should be reduced.

The jobs emphasis was welcome.

More state and local control *may* be a good idea.

But Congress tried to reform welfare and slash funding at the same time, even though early Republican-led efforts at the state level, such as the one in Wisconsin, confirmed that in the short run moving people off welfare costs substantially more, not less, per client. The higher cost comes from the need for transitional assistance in education, job training, child care, health insurance and transportation. Yet the national welfare reform act took $54 billion away from low-income people over a six-year period. That's equivalent to more than $1,500 for every child, woman and man who lives under the poverty line.

The rush to slash assistance prompted one syndicated columnist to write, "What's missing is the sense that poverty has anything to do with our own fundamental humanity, with who and what we are—and ought to be. That may not be the same thing as turning our backs on the poor, but it's hard to tell the difference."[2]

Doesn't the idea of being on assistance go against the American tradition of rugged individualism?

Sure. For most people, accepting assistance is the last resort. But wait! What kind of assistance are you talking about? For some reason it's *poverty* assistance that's considered shameful, though vastly greater sums assist affluent citizens. You don't mind taking an interest deduction on your home mortgage, do you? If you are a student, you may be willing to take out a government-backed loan to attend a government-supported college or university. If you are retired, you willingly collect Social Security or get Medicare coverage, even though the benefits far exceed what you've paid into those programs. Our government provides billions of dollars a year to farms and businesses—"corporate welfare," according to Representative John Kasich, chairman of the Budget Committee in the U.S. House of Representatives.

In 1993, tax deductions, credits and deferrals cost the federal government an estimated $400 billion in revenues, equivalent to 29 percent of federal government spending. The eight largest of these were deductions for mortgage interest, capital gains, pension contributions and earnings, real estate taxes, state and local taxes, charitable contributions, medical expenses and employer health insurance contributions that, together, totaled $216 billion. One-third of these benefits went to the wealthiest 5 percent of taxpayers, while just 7 percent went to the bottom 52 percent.

That same year, the federal government spent nearly $600 billion on programs that mainly benefit middle-class and wealthy people. These include Medicare, Social Security, government retirement benefits, Unemployment Compensation, farm price supports and veterans' benefits. This spending accounted for nearly 43 percent of federal outlays.

In contrast, all federal spending on benefits for poor and near-poor people amounted to $162 billion, or 12 percent of federal outlays, and went to 26 percent of the U.S. population. That included not only welfare, but also guaranteed student loans, Medicaid, food stamps, child nutrition programs, the Earned Income Tax Credit (EITC), Supplemental Security Income for disabled and elderly people and Child Support Enforcement. Forty percent of those receiving assistance were children, and 43 percent lived below the poverty line.[3]

Haven't government antipoverty programs fostered abuse, dependency and irresponsibility?

The abuse is far less costly and may be less widespread than, for example, cheating among upper- and middle-income people on their income tax. Under the old welfare system, some recipients did become dependent, even for generations, but 70 percent were short-termers—parents who used welfare in an emergency and left within two years.[4] As for irresponsibility, there is no evidence, for example, that welfare encourages teen pregnancies. On the contrary, teenage pregnancies are more common in states where welfare benefits are low.

Now a major nationwide effort is under way to root out dependency and irresponsibility among the income recipients of public assistance. The authors think that much good, as well as harm, will come of this effort, but wish an equally vigorous effort would be mounted to overcome hunger.

Is letting state and local governments run welfare a good idea?

We'll have to see. In principle, the federal government should not do what smaller units of society can do well. But this principle has to pass the test of reality. In the United States the reason for federal leadership in assistance was the inability or unwillingness of many state and local governments to respond adequately. Sometimes the more local the institution, the more it has discriminated against racial or economically vulnerable groups. Welfare reform is now giving state and local governments a major opportunity to show what they can do. But the federal government should reinstate minimum standards and provide funding so that no one in the United States goes hungry, whether that child lives in Mississippi or Minnesota.

How is welfare reform working in practice?

That varies from state to state. Early reports have been quite mixed. One positive outcome of welfare reform could be a new partnership between governments and local initiatives. A host of innovative efforts to reduce hunger and poverty is under way. Typically, local leaders often draw on some government funding or support, and many will come up with ideas about how federal and state governments could be more helpful. Bill Ayres, the head of World Hunger Year, calls this "policy from the grass roots up." The "charitable choice" provision in the welfare act of 1996, developed in part by a nonpartisan Christian policy institute, the Center for Public Justice, encourages state governments to fund private assistance efforts and allows explicitly faith-based programs to compete for funding—as long as people who need help can freely choose between religious and nonreligious programs. Valuable lessons about what works will emerge from the new partnerships that are being formed.

On the other hand, welfare recipients are required by federal law to find employment within two years and face a five-year lifetime limit on benefits. Some states have imposed more stringent limits. Many welfare recipients are ill-educated and unskilled and live in areas where the unemployment rate makes work difficult to find. What if the most poorly equipped job seekers can't get or keep jobs? What will happen to them and their children? Will we let them freeze or starve?

According to a 1998 study by the Center on Hunger, Poverty and Nutrition Policy at Tufts University, 35 of the 50 states have implemented state welfare policies that will make the economic situations of families worse than under the old welfare system.[5] This was surprising, because the welfare law of 1996 gave states increased federal subsidies in the early years of a five-year period, with less to be given later. In addition, state coffers had been overflowing, thanks to a strong economy. So it seems likely that states will further cut spending to reduce hunger and poverty in the coming years, unless voters speak up for a different outcome.

What can people do?

Citizens need to monitor this massive social experiment carefully and then urge legislatures and Congress to make necessary changes. Bread for the World Institute has been helping local leaders in a number of states form state-level hunger coalitions.[6] It is more important than ever that antihunger advocates influence the decisions of state legislatures about welfare and related programs. In Alabama, for example, a strong advocacy organization, Alabama Arise, helped win state welfare policies that are more favorable toward poor and hungry people than those of neighboring states.[7]

Few people want to return to the old welfare system, but the United States needs a second generation of welfare reform that will help people who now sometimes go hungry to move out of poverty. That kind of welfare reform would cost more than the current system but would save money in the long run, as people make a productive contribution to the work force, no longer require assistance and begin paying taxes. In addition, the social dividend—millions of fulfilled lives, more hopeful children, less crime—would be incalculable.

Gender
and
Race

Chapter 13
Women Bear the Brunt

Efriendi Bea is a poor wife and mother in rural Indonesia. Even though Efriendi is pregnant and due to give birth in a few weeks, her diet lately has consisted of only bark and roots gleaned from trees in the woods.

"When we get some meat, my husband eats it," says Efriendi. "My husband has to work hard, farming and fishing, so he takes the meat so he'll have energy."[1]

"Living with him was very hard. I never knew when he'd get mad. He'd come home in the middle of the night and start hitting me. The night I left, he was hitting me. My son who was four then was running down the street, yelling, 'You have to call the police, my daddy is hitting my mom.' We went to The Spring in Tampa. There I had one twin bed and one crib for all of us and we shared the room with another woman and her two kids. The people at The Spring got me into this housing project.

"I spent the first month crying every day. I didn't know what to do— all I'd ever been was a wife and mother since I was fourteen. And I'd never been around some of the kinds of people who were at the shelter before.

"I have good days and bad days. I feel guilty for bringing the kids into this situation, especially when we have cereal for dinner."

—A single mother in Florida[2]

In most countries, women do not usually have as much power, money or education as men. Because of this, women are more likely to go hungry. Since women are responsible for most child care, the advancement of women improves health and reduces hunger among children.

Does the gap between what women and men earn contribute to hunger?

Around the world, women work outside the home to provide for themselves and for their families. They labor in fields under the blazing sun, by the sides of dusty roads, in factories and in office buildings, but their work is valued far less than that of men. Accordingly, they are paid less and more often go hungry. Any strategy to reduce hunger should include efforts to eliminate discrimination against women and improve their job prospects.

On average, women receive 30 to 40 percent less than men for comparable work.[3] In the United States, women average about 24 percent less than men for full-time wage and salary work. In addition, throughout the world, women typically do most of the work at home, but they don't get paid for it, and it is sometimes not even recognized as work.

What other forms of discrimination do women face?

Custom and law often hold women back. African women produce up to 80 percent of the food, but in much of Africa a woman's access to land is determined by marital status and the number of sons she has.[4] In some countries, a woman cannot legally own land.

In many families girls and women are the last in line, not just for food but for medical care as well.[5] In Asian countries, when a son gets sick, a poor family is more likely to take him to a doctor; daughters sometimes get ignored or put to bed. They are told they will feel better the next day. In many societies, women are conditioned not to complain, but to adapt in silence. Babies and small children share in the underfeeding and relative neglect their mothers endure.

Amartya Sen, the Nobel Prize-winning economist, notes that the population of the developing countries includes about 100 million fewer girls and women than would be expected. Often deprived of food and medicine, women and girls suffer higher mortality rates. India and China, where gender-biased abortions are also prevalent, account for most of the "missing" women.[6]

As the ones whose bodies carry, deliver and nurse children, women have specific nutritional needs and health risks. Worldwide, anemia afflicts 48 percent of pregnant women, and nearly 600 thousand women, most in developing countries, die every year from pregnancy-related causes. An African woman is 500 times more likely to die from such causes than a woman in a Scandinavian country.[7]

4 a.m.	Fish in local pond
6 a.m.	Light fire, heat washing water, cook breakfast, wash dishes, sweep compound
8 a.m.	Work in rice fields with two children, carrying one on her back
11 a.m.	Collect berries, leaves and bark, carry water
12 p.m.	Process and prepare food, cook lunch, wash dishes
2 p.m.	Wash clothes, carry water, clean and smoke fish
3 p.m.	Work in home garden
5 p.m.	Fish in local pond
6 p.m.	Process and prepare food, cook dinner
8 p.m.	Wash dishes, bathe children
9 p.m.	Shell seeds and make fishnets while conversing
11 p.m.	around fire

A woman's day in Sierra Leone

Source: FAO, Women Feed the World, *(Rome; FAO, 1998), 2.*

Some women also suffer physical abuse. Ina Ako sells chilies in Waikabubak, Indonesia. She is afraid because her husband beats her when she doesn't have enough food to feed him. She says, "When there's no food, the men get very angry."[8] In the United States, many women have settled for welfare or worse in order to escape domestic violence.

In the United States, are women more likely than men to go hungry?

Sixty-three percent of all U.S. adults in poverty are women.[9] Women suffer hunger and poverty in disproportionate numbers partly because they earn lower wages.

The increase in single-parent families is also a factor. As out-of-wedlock births and divorce have become more prevalent, the share of poor people who are women has increased. The trend toward single-parent families has affected all income groups, not just poor people. But many women are pushed into poverty when they have to support children on their own.

A single-parent household is four times more likely to suffer hunger than a two-parent household.[10] Only half of the single parents who had child support awarded and due receive the full amount. About a quarter receive partial payment and a quarter receive nothing at all.[11] The great majority of single households are headed by women.

Fostering stable marriages can help to reduce hunger and poverty among women. Churches, of course, encourage people to raise children within stable marriages. Organizations such as the Christian Coalition and Focus on the Family have been forceful in bringing a concern for family values into U.S. politics. At times, these organizations have focused on abortion, homosexuality and opposition to government assistance. They have largely failed to defend hungry and poor people, a shortcoming that is neither biblical nor contributes to the strengthening of families. But they and other conservative groups have also helped win support for some promising proposals—such as tougher child support enforcement and modifications in state marriage laws.[12]

What can be done to counteract discrimination against women worldwide?

Focusing on the education of women and especially girls is one approach. The World Bank considers the improvement of girls' education to be the single most important investment that a developing country can make because it has "a catalytic effect on every dimension of development. . . ."[13] That includes better health, better nutrition, higher income and higher crop yields. Yet many parents and politicians around the world consider schooling for girls a waste of time. The impact of this bias can be seen in adult literacy rates. Among the 900 million illiterate people in the developing world, women still outnumber men by almost two to one.[14]

Including women in development projects is another way to counteract discrimination. In 1988 Bread for the World drafted legislation and launched a major campaign on *Women in Develop-*

ment to address the fact that the U.S. Agency for International Development (USAID) programs were largely bypassing women. Many people asked, "Why is Bread for the World moving away from its focus on hunger?" Bread for the World was *not* moving away from hunger. It chose that target because of the great impact that the treatment of women has on hunger. By compelling USAID to fully include women at every stage and in every facet of the development process in its projects, the legislation has benefited countless struggling families. It also helped set a high standard for other development agencies regarding the inclusion of women.

In most households around the world, women prepare food for their families. Yet they often receive less than a fair share of the family's food and other resources, and their deprivation limits what they can do for their children.

Lifting barriers against women is essential to progress against hunger.

Chapter 14

Racism and Hunger

> I truly understand that God shows no partiality, but in every nation anyone who fears him and does what is right is acceptable to him.   —*Peter, Acts 10:34–35*

Racism exists all over the world. It is a piece of the same cloth as ethnic, gender or religious discrimination. Because it erects obstacles and denies opportunities, one of its ugly consequences is to push people into hunger and poverty.

Consider this nation. Though it was founded on the ideal that all people are equal, endowed by their Creator with the right to liberty, vast numbers of Africans were torn from their families, enslaved and forcibly exported to the United States or its predecessor colonies. Slaves were eventually emancipated, but without land, money or education it was extremely difficult for them to survive. In addition they faced a largely hostile society and servile conditions that were reinforced by racial segregation throughout the South and in much of the North. In the 1950s and 1960s, African Americans finally secured their civil rights. Since then, many African Americans have made enormous progress. But the lag between promise and reality is still apparent because it is not possible to put people at the bottom of the pile for a few centuries and then expect that they will suddenly have the same chance as others.

The Reverend Don Williams, director of racial-ethnic church relations at Bread for the World, recently made this comment to the authors: "We now have, just in our lifetime, the right to vote. We can now go to a hotel, a movie, a restaurant or ride public transportation. But that does not close the 340-year gap that exists between blacks and whites in almost every area."

The legacy of racism is apparent in the fact that, proportionally, three times as many African Americans live in poverty (27%) as white Americans (9%).[1] This imbalance reflects a lag in the education and training of African Americans, as well as a higher incidence of broken homes and crime and substance abuse in the African American community.

But hunger and poverty among African Americans reflect present as well as past racial obstacles. Some of these obstacles stem from prejudice. Some injustices have simply been built into "the way things work" and are perpetuated even where no malice is intended. Just as advantages usually get passed from one generation to the next, so do disadvantages.

Are the same dynamics at work regarding racism outside the United States?

Unfortunately they are. South Africa, which also had a cruel system of segregation (apartheid), is a case in point. As of 1990, white South Africans, who made up 13 percent of the population, owned 85 percent of the land; the black majority was forced to eke out a living on patches of marginal soil. Stripped of rights and opportunities, South Africa's black population was impoverished. Not surprisingly, hunger and malnutrition were prevalent among blacks.[2]

In May 1994, after 27 years of imprisonment, Nelson Mandela became the first president of a truly democratic South Africa. However, the advent of a multiracial democracy did not wipe out the economic disparity created by decades of apartheid. According to the United Nations Development Program, which uses a Human Development Index to measure the relative well-being of the world's countries, white South Africa (if considered as a separate country) ranked 23d among all nations. But black South Africa, considered separately, ranked a hundred countries lower, at 123d.[3] The legacy of racism is not easily undone, even with the best of intentions. And since prejudice and selfishness linger in the human heart, the best of intentions cannot be assumed.

From the struggles of Native Americans to ethnic rivalries in the former Yugoslavia, from tribal killings in Rwanda and Burundi to tension between Hindus and Muslims in India, from the Holocaust during World War II to violence against ethnic Chinese in Indonesia—all exhibit how hatred can coalesce around human differences and sometimes spawn violence that leaves generations of poverty in its wake.

For these reasons, anything that can be done to further racial healing and racial justice will contribute measurably to the reduction of hunger. The reverse is also true: reductions in hunger and poverty contribute to racial healing and justice, because they address some of the worst inequities.

But can the link between hunger and race be documented?

It has been documented. Although the largest number of poor and hungry people in the United States are white (simply because non-Hispanic white people make up 71 percent of the population), poverty and hunger *rates* are much higher for several other groups.

	Percent in poverty[4]	Percent food insecure[5]	Estimated percent with moderate to severe hunger[6]
White Americans	9	11	3
African Americans	27	25	9
Hispanics	27	28	9
Asian Americans	14	N/A	N/A

What other indicators are there of racial disparities in the United States that might have an impact on hunger?

- The unemployment rate in 1997 for white Americans was 4 percent, for African Americans 10 percent, for Hispanics 8 percent and for Asian Americans 5 percent.[7]
- The average family income for white Americans was $39,000, for African Americans $25,000, for Hispanics $27,000 and for Asian Americans $45,000.[8]
- The poverty rate for white American children was 16 percent, for African American children 37 percent, for Hispanic children 37 percent and for Asian American children 20 percent.[9]
- For more than a generation the Pine Ridge Indian Reservation in South Dakota has been the nation's most impoverished jurisdiction.

Amartya Sen has shown that the mortality rate for U.S. African Americans is higher than the mortality rate for people in China or the state of Kerala in India. The mortality rate for African American men in Harlem is higher than the death rate for men in Bangladesh.[10]

Does racism affect economic opportunity? If the economy is strong, can't anyone get a job or start a business by just putting his or her mind to it and working hard?

Many African Americans and Latinos are succeeding in the job market and in business. But people of color often have to overcome obstacles. For example, African Americans find it harder to win small-business bank loans than their white counterparts. Discrimination in the real estate market still means that African Americans are discouraged from living in many communities. Farms owned by African Americans have been disappearing at a rate nearly four times that of farms owned by white Americans, and African American farmers have shown that U.S. Department of Agriculture loans were often withheld from them despite a policy of nondiscrimination. These persistent difficulties hold people back and increase the incidence of hunger and poverty.

Since prejudice is hard to eradicate, what can be done?

Prejudice is a stain on the heart that the law cannot remove. The law can, however, have an impact on actions and attitudes. The civil rights rulings and laws during the 1950s and 1960s had a great deal to do with bringing about a sea change in our culture regarding race. Studies have shown that younger people in the United States are far less shaped by racial prejudice today than their parents and grandparents were. Much of the change was driven, as in the case of Martin Luther King, Jr., by people of faith; so faith was a big factor in this process.

Regarding the matter of prejudice, the authors believe that the most powerful tool is the gospel of Christ. That gospel changes hearts and unites us as brothers and sisters, children of the same God and Savior. In Christ there is no slave or free, male or female, black, yellow, red or white; all are united and equal. And in Christ we have the gift of forgiveness that sets us free from bondage to the hatreds of the world and reconciles us to one another.

Disadvantages are another matter. Faith does not provide an instant education or job skills. But it does provide hope in God and purpose for life, which become forces for opening up possibilities, including those of getting an education and job skills or seeing to it that your children do. So Christians rightly regard the celebration and sharing of faith as the most constructive contribution that might be offered to those who are disadvantaged. But faith without works is dead (Jas 2:14–26), and Christians also see the ordering of society as having the God-given purpose of bringing about public justice. That's what the civil rights movement was about.

So how can public justice be achieved for those who, partly as the heritage of slavery, find themselves facing hunger and poverty?

One way is by improving the economic situation of everyone. When people have jobs, food, stability and the belief that the improvement of their lives is possible, there is less of a tendency to scapegoat those who are perceived as different. Another part of the answer is to focus on work incentives, opportunities and support services for those who are struggling. Special efforts, such as affirmative action, to include historically disadvantaged groups can also help.

Could you be more specific?

Take a young male—black, white, Hispanic, whatever—perhaps a school dropout who lives in a poor neighborhood and has gotten most of his training in the street. Maybe he has no father to give him the guidance he needs. He's a ripe candidate for drug use, for the commission of various other crimes, for siring children to whom he can hardly be a suitable father, and for destitution. He needs help. Now the government alone can't provide the help he needs. His family alone cannot do so. The church could play a key part if one or more members cared enough to draw him into fellowship. But the church alone can't do it all, either. Each of these could play a role in the salvaging of this young man.

One thing readers of this book, some of whom would have little opportunity to relate to such a man personally, can do is to see to it that public justice is there for him—not just in the courts and prisons after he gets into trouble, but in the job opportunities, training and encouragement that he needs to share in the American dream and stay out of trouble. This requires citizens who care enough to seek government policies that provide opportunities, even if such policies would be to their financial disadvantage in the short term. Such efforts, along with personal intervention, are a part of racial healing and an important step toward ending hunger.

How else can Christians respond to racial inequity?

By continuing to live the faith in love, by making churches examples of interracial fellowship and by speaking out against prejudice. Christians can also become members of a group such as Bread for the World, which actively includes people of all races in its staff, board and membership and works to get everyone a place at the table. Some Christians were at the forefront of the antislavery movement of the 1800s, the remarkable postslavery collaboration of freed blacks and whites during Reconstruction and the civil rights movement in the twentieth century. But in each case, the majority of Christians were passive, and some supported the existing culture of oppression. We can follow the example of those who had the courage to be racial healers and, in so doing, contribute to the end of hunger as well.

The Economics
of
Hunger

WARNING:

*This section gets a little more complicated
and is intended for readers who want to tackle
the more complex side of hunger.*

*Those of you who prefer to stick to simple
but effective ways of reducing hunger
may wish to skip to Section VII,
"The Politics of Hunger."*

Chapter 15

Two Cheers for Capitalism

> The central irony of our time . . . is this: A capitalist society depends on noncapitalist values in order to hold together and prosper.
> —*E. J. Dionne*[1]

Is free-market capitalism the cause of hunger or the solution?

The free-market system is a huge part of the solution because it expands production and organizes most of the world's employment. It is not the whole solution, however, and left entirely to its own devices it will leave many people hungry.

Why is free enterprise such an impressive engine of growth?

Under the free-market system, business and industry have to respond to consumer demand in order to make a profit. The terms *business* and *industry* can refer to someone collecting and selling junk or to a multinational bank, to a child raising chickens or to an auto manufacturer. Enterprise is *free* in the sense of giving people freedom and incentives to develop products and sell them on the open market. This encourages innovation and hard work.

Why, then, do capitalism and free enterprise come under so much criticism?

Because of the excesses and inequalities that capitalism fosters. Put another way, free enterprise is a superb engine of growth, but an engine is not a steering wheel. Free enterprise by itself does not answer questions about what sort of society we aspire to be or how we can enable everyone to have a stake in the economy.

It is morally neutral and does not distinguish between drug trafficking and selling Bibles.

In a free-market system, demand for food stimulates its production and distribution. But *demand* refers to purchasing power. If you need food but don't have money, you go hungry.

How can that be dealt with?

The free-market system needs guidance. For example, environmental regulations reduce industrial pollution. It would be difficult for one company to implement environmental standards on its own. Its costs would go up, and it would lose business to competitors. So, responding to public demand, the government enacts laws that make all companies reduce pollution. That levels the playing field, while requiring some social responsibility.

Taxation provides another way of making capitalism more socially responsible. Taxes pay for national defense, highways, schools, research, parks and playgrounds, police and fire departments, courts and many other things that protect or improve the quality of life. Taxes can also serve to blunt the extremes between rich and poor by taxing large incomes at a higher rate than low incomes and using some of the revenue for such things as medical insurance and job training.

Endless debates rage about how much governments should intervene. Too much intervention or the wrong kind can stifle growth, and no one wants to harm a goose that's laying golden eggs. State-controlled development can also be even rougher on the environment than unrestrained capitalism, as the nuclear accident at Chernobyl and widespread environmental devastation in the former Soviet Union show. Yet, no country tolerates unrestrained capitalism. The 1980s and 1990s saw a worldwide trend toward more reliance on markets, but each country mixes reliance on government and markets in a distinctive way.

What are some of the variations?

Let's start with China. China's communist rulers were shrewd enough to rescue the economy by turning to free enterprise. China's economy has expanded at the astounding rate of almost

10 percent a year during most of the 1990s. But while China's economy is now largely driven by private enterprise, state-owned firms still account for about a third of the country's output. They tend to be inefficient, propped up by government subsidies and bank loans, many of which may never be repaid. The government is gradually privatizing many of these publicly owned firms.

In Russia, the sudden collapse of communism has left its citizens in a far worse situation than the one faced by the people of the United States during the Great Depression. The old system fell apart, and Russians suddenly had to build a new one from the wreckage. Russia has been trying to put in place a framework of laws and practices for free enterprise, but meanwhile great distortions have developed, with some former communist officials, among others, virtually stealing parts of the economy and emerging as born-again capitalists. In ways reminiscent of the Wild West and the robber-baron era in the United States, a few have made fortunes, while the many have become more impoverished. Collapse of the ruble in 1998 added to economic uncertainty—and poverty—in Russia.

Isn't western Europe also becoming more capitalist?

All the nations of western Europe have stronger social welfare systems than the United States. Over the last decade, most European nations have scaled back these systems to keep them affordable and give people more incentive to be productive. But none of these nations is seriously considering dismantling its social welfare system. Most Europeans prefer their socialized systems of medicine and generous unemployment insurance to the hard-edged economic system of the United States.

And the developing countries?

Many countries in Asia, Africa and Latin America have also moved away from socialist ideas toward more reliance on markets. This is partly because foreign aid agencies and the International Monetary Fund have insisted on free-market reforms as a condition for aid and loans. It is also because many of the ambitious governmental schemes of prior decades simply did not work. But scaling back on the size and scope of government has also thrown some people out of work and reduced social services. In most countries, the gap between rich and poor has widened.

What about the impact of capitalism on culture?

People all over the world are now bombarded with commercial advertisements. Sophisticated propaganda techniques are used to convince people that they really need the things that money can buy—that the quality of life depends mainly on getting and spending. The religious impact of commercial advertising is pervasive and pernicious.

In more affluent countries, most families are devoting more time to making money. Both spouses typically work, partly because people feel they need things that their parents considered luxuries. An array of attractive ways to spend money keeps people on the go. Many people wonder whether their lives are too busy, but few people decide to simplify their lives and slow down.

One side effect is that most affluent people feel that they cannot afford to increase their charitable giving or give more time to civic affairs. The precious energy God has given is poured out in service of mammon.

The irony is that capitalism works best when people in business are honest and committed to being of real service to their customers. Capitalism is most attractive when it is balanced by democratic government and a strong sector of religious, humanitarian and civic activity. Keeping the balance is quite a challenge, one made more complex by a new reality: the globalization of the economy.

Chapter 16

The Global Economy

> For breakfast this morning I enjoyed orange juice from Florida, tea from South Asia and a banana from Central America on cereal manufactured in Michigan from grains grown somewhere in the Midwest or Plains states. After breakfast, I put on clothes sewn in the Dominican Republic, Guatemala, Bangladesh and Zimbabwe. My new sneakers were assembled in China, in contrast to the five-year-old pair—same brand and model—which was sewn in Korea. Nothing in today's breakfast or wardrobe was made in my Maryland suburb of Washington, D.C. Only my raincoat was assembled within the state of Maryland, and that factory just closed.
>
> *—Don Reeves*[1]

The world is now knit together by the global market economy. Affluent North Americans are linked together with very poor people around the world by trade, investment and migration. The global market economy is spurring economic growth, helping some people to get rich and many to escape from hunger, but it is leaving millions of poor people far behind and making many poorer than they were. Worldwide economic growth also adds to the overload on earth's natural resources.

The global market economy is likely to dominate the world for the foreseeable future. Those who want to reduce hunger need to learn about it and push for policies that will make it work better for hungry people. Bread for the World Institute has focused much of its recent research on how policies toward the global economy affect hungry people.

The global economy has been around for a long time. So what's new?

The scale of international trade and investment is bigger than ever, and the collapse of communism has brought the world into one global market. The global economy has replaced the Cold War as the overarching international fact of life.

Today's global economy has its roots in Europe's conquest of much of the rest of the world. Long after colonialism has ended, some of its economic structures persist. Development is oriented toward rich-country markets, and it is sometimes controlled from rich-country offices.

Before World War I, trade and investment flowed across national borders as freely as today. War and economic problems led to trade barriers, which contributed to the global depression of the 1930s. The global depression, in turn, contributed to political extremes and the outbreak of World War II.

After World War II, steps were taken to ensure a more open international economy. That economic order, along with technological advances, generated vast new economic growth in the industrial north and many developing countries. In fact, the economic expansion that occurred in the second half of the twentieth century is without precedent.

Trade barriers have been steadily reduced. Cross-border investments have increased. Thanks to rapid advances in computer and communications technologies, investors are now active simultaneously in stock markets around the world. Banking, too, has been more fully internationalized. Cash transactions across borders exceed a trillion dollars a day.

Is the globalization of economies a good thing?

Overall, the globalization of the economy makes production and distribution more efficient and dynamic, bringing economic gains to the world.

But global competition has two edges. One edge stimulates growth, wealth and employment. It creates winners. The winners include most of the people in the United States as well as many people in developing countries who have new opportunities to lift themselves out of hunger and poverty. The other edge creates losers, including many less educated U.S. workers and many nations that, for one reason or another, have been unable to keep up with rapid changes in the global economy. Expanding production and trade also have environmental costs, and the

global mobility of capital makes it harder for individual governments to maintain social and environmental standards.

What is the impact of the global economy on hunger?

Global commerce has contributed to economic growth, without
which hunger would have greatly increased. Hunger and poverty
have declined most in regions that have been deeply engaged in
the global economy—East Asia, southern Europe and the Middle
East. On the other hand, the gap between rich and poor countries, as well as between rich and poor people within many
countries, is enormous and has widened.

The three richest people in the world have assets that exceed
the combined national income of the 48 least developed countries. The world's 225 richest individuals (of whom 60 are U.S.
citizens) have total assets of over one trillion dollars—equal to
the annual income of the bottom half of the world's population.[2]

The gap in average per capita income between the industrial
and developing worlds has widened from $5,700 in 1960 to
$17,000 in 1995. Many of the poorest countries in the world are
falling behind. In more than 100 countries, income per capita
was lower in 1998 than it was 15 years earlier. In Africa, total
consumption was 20 percent lower than in 1980.[3]

Groups of people that are not quick to seize opportunities in
the global economy suffer declines in income. In Tanzania, for
example, farmers face falling prices for their coffee partly because
farmers in far-off Malaysia have found ways to produce coffee
more efficiently.

Doesn't the global economy put inordinate power in the hands of multinational corporations?

Multinationals do have extraordinary power. The world's 40
thousand transnational corporations (TNCs) account for most of
the movement of goods, services and funds across national borders. One-third of world trade consists of transactions among
various units of single corporations.[4] The combined sales of the
200 largest TNCs represent approximately 29 percent of global
economic activity, though they employ less than one percent of
the global work force.

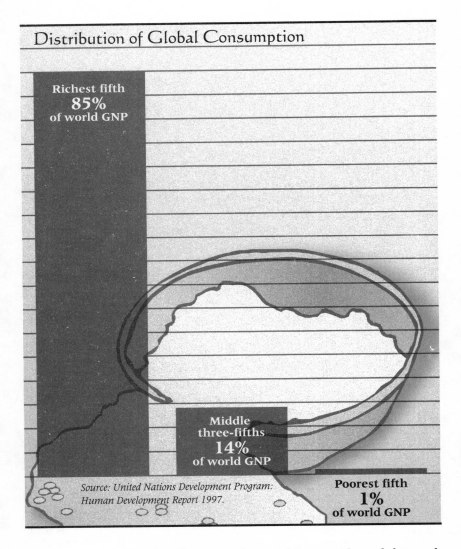

Distribution of Global Consumption

Richest fifth
85%
of world GNP

Middle
three-fifths
14%
of world GNP

Poorest fifth
1%
of world GNP

Source: United Nations Development Program: Human Development Report 1997.

TNCs offer efficiencies in matching supply and demand, product quality and some of the best research and development of technologies. But big corporations can also use their money and size to sway political decisions in their favor. In the United States, for example, political action committees (PACs) often win

State and corporate power,
Total GDP or corporate sales, 1994
(US$ billions)

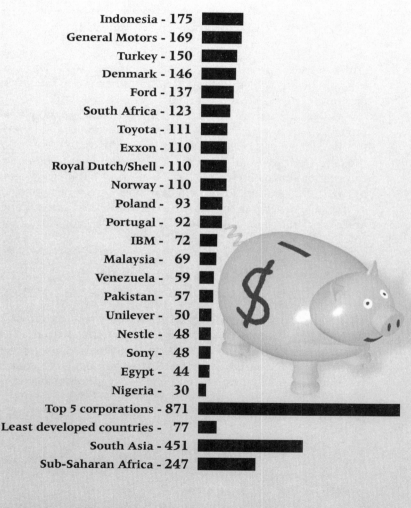

Indonesia - **175**	
General Motors - **169**	
Turkey - **150**	
Denmark - **146**	
Ford - **137**	
South Africa - **123**	
Toyota - **111**	
Exxon - **110**	
Royal Dutch/Shell - **110**	
Norway - **110**	
Poland - **93**	
Portugal - **92**	
IBM - **72**	
Malaysia - **69**	
Venezuela - **59**	
Pakistan - **57**	
Unilever - **50**	
Nestle - **48**	
Sony - **48**	
Egypt - **44**	
Nigeria - **30**	
Top 5 corporations - **871**	
Least developed countries - **77**	
South Asia - **451**	
Sub-Saharan Africa - **247**	

Sources: Fortune *Magazine 1996, World Bank 1995 and UNRISD 1995*

political favors for particular industries or companies. Big companies can insist that state governments or developing-country governments give them tax breaks or special favors that may not be in the public interest.

What can be done to capitalize on the advantages of the global economy and moderate its downsides?

The global economy makes it all the more urgent for each government to ensure that working people earn a livable wage, to invest in health and education for all and to maintain safety-net programs.

Governments can also act together to manage the global economy for the benefit of all. International standards—to protect basic labor rights, for example, or the environment—make it easier for individual governments to maintain safeguards. International institutions (such as the World Bank or agencies of the United Nations) can help developing countries promote sustainable development and reduce poverty. The United States and other large, affluent countries dominate decisions about the rules and institutions of the global economy.

Will governments do what they can to make the global economy work better for hungry people?

That's not clear. The global-market economy adds to the pressure on each government to give free rein to business in order to attract companies that might otherwise move somewhere else. In the United States, corporate taxes dropped from 30 percent of revenues in 1960 to three percent in 1995.[5] Multinational corporations also make sure their interests are well represented in international negotiations regarding trade and other aspects of global commerce.

But in democracies, government will do as citizens insist. Concerned citizens need to focus on global economic issues and demand justice for hungry people. Failure to do so is to turn hungry people away from the table.

Chapter 17

Does Trade Hurt or Help?

All of us learned the advantages and risks of trade when we were kids.

"I'll give you a bag of marbles for your game," a child says. And if the marbles are worth more than the game to the child's friend, both emerge winners.

On a much vaster scale international trade offers the same possibility. It widens the opportunities for product and service development as well as for the expansion of jobs and income.

How does international trade help hungry people?

Exports can contribute powerfully to economic growth. A World Bank study of nations from 1987 to 1993 found that poverty rates did not decline in any country where there was not economic growth.[1]

While foreign aid is still needed, trade has a much bigger impact on a developing country's well-being. In 1996, even the low-income developing countries received more than $300 billion from exports, compared to $28 billion from development assistance.[2]

But trade is a harsh taskmaster. It is tough to compete internationally, especially for poor countries. Also, exports and economic growth do not always lead to less hunger and poverty. They do so only when the benefits are broadly shared as part of a development strategy that brings jobs and opportunity to people who would otherwise go hungry.

What does it take to expand exports?

It takes businesses that spot export opportunities, develop them and then work hard to stay competitive. Governments can sometimes help most by *not* intervening—by reducing tariffs (which block imports and indirectly discourage exports) and currency restrictions. When a country's economy is not doing well, its government sometimes will refuse to let its currency be traded freely. That props up the official value of the currency, but also makes the country's exports more expensive and harder to sell.

Some countries don't have much to sell that the world wants to buy. How can they get ahead by exporting?

Low wages allow poor countries to produce some things inexpensively, and some poor countries also have raw materials. Unfortunately, the terms of trade have generally become less favorable for countries that depend on low-cost labor and raw materials. Educated workers figure out smarter ways of doing things, and synthetic materials are being improved all the time. So the wages of uneducated workers and the prices of raw materials have lagged behind the prices for high-tech goods.

Poor countries must try to adapt to change by educating their workforce, spotting new uses for unskilled labor and raw materials and developing their capacity to process their raw materials. But even countries that can't keep up with global change are likely to do better by staying engaged in international trade than by throwing up high barriers to imports and exports. Trade exposes the country to new ideas and technologies, while extensive regulation of trade sets up lots of temptations to bribery and corruption.

Why should countries grow crops for export if their people are hungry? Isn't that self-defeating?

It can be. Landless people sometimes go hungry within view of plantations devoted to coffee or strawberries grown for rich people in other countries.

If only a few people are enriched by an export, emphasis on export crops will increase hunger. But if many people are employed by the exporters, and some of the income from export earnings is used for education, basic health care and job development, export crops can be an effective means to reduce hunger. Kenya's attempt at export crop promotion has failed to reduce hunger because it has mainly benefited plantation farmers and transnational corporations, and under President Daniel Arap Moi's increasingly authoritarian rule, equity has not been a high priority. School attendance has declined, especially in rural areas and among girls. Between 1970 and 1991, the proportion of chronically undernourished people in Kenya increased from 33 to 46 percent. Most of this cannot be blamed on export cropping, but export cropping played a role in the larger pattern of poor development policies.

During the same period, Costa Rica rapidly expanded production of fruits, vegetables, ornamental plants and flowers for export, mostly to the United States. By 1994 these products accounted for 42 percent of Costa Rica's export earnings. The initiative created jobs, especially for women, boosted rural income and improved rural living standards, and income from the exports helped pay for food imports. Costa Rica's commitment to education, health care, land reform, public works employment, social insurance, democracy and low military spending helped make the move toward export crop promotion beneficial to the nation. While chronic undernourishment increased in Kenya, Costa Rica reduced it from 25 percent in 1970 to 12 percent in 1991.[3]

Doesn't the global economy make it hard for workers to bargain and drive down wages everywhere?

In a globally competitive market, jobs are a bit like water seeking the lowest available level. Industries will tend to move where the conditions are most attractive. Among the most powerful attractions is a diligent workforce willing to work for low wages. Workers in poor countries may put up with terrible conditions because the alternative for them—often unemployment or grueling subsistence agriculture—is even worse. Workers everywhere are pitted against each other.

But global competition also gives opportunities to poor people in developing countries. As several decades of industrial development in Taiwan and South Korea illustrate, people may start working for low wages in apparel factories, improve their standard of living as well as their levels of education and training, and then move to higher-wage jobs in more technically advanced industries. As wage levels and living standards rise, apparel manufacturers then relocate to a lower-wage country and begin the process again.

How can U.S. trade policies and international agreements make trade work better for hungry people?

For the sake of low-income people in the United States, freer trade should be complemented by steps to enhance the domestic job market, improve education and strengthen the U.S. social safety net. Otherwise, increased competition from low-wage countries will add to growing wage inequality in our own country. In addition, workers displaced by trade should be offered special help to retrain or relocate.

But the United States should reduce the barriers it maintains against those developing-country imports that compete with U.S. products. The industrial countries still tightly restrict imports of simple manufactured goods like clothing and shoes. These restrictions block the entry of very poor countries into manufacturing and slow down the graduation of developing countries toward more sophisticated manufacturing. The United States also restricts imports of some agricultural products, such as sugar, that can also be produced domestically.

The latest round of international trade agreements included a commitment to reducing restrictions on textiles and tropical crops within the round's ten-year term. But the industrial countries are permitted to delay most of the reduction until the end of the period, and there is some chance that some countries will then renege on their commitment.[4]

Reducing industrial-country barriers to developing-country imports by half would, by one estimate, be worth about as much as all the development aid the developing countries receive.[5] Aid is still necessary, especially for low-income countries and poverty reduction efforts. But trade opportunities are also important to progress against hunger.

In a competitive global economy, what rights do workers have?

Nearly all nations have agreed in principle on some basic labor rights—no abusive child labor, no slavery, and, most important, the right of workers to form unions. But these rights are widely ignored.

Michelle Tooley, a professor of religion at Belmont University and a Bread for the World board member, reported on conditions she witnessed during a 1996 trip to Nicaragua:

In Nicaragua, runaway unemployment makes practically any kind of job a luxury. Thus it is that 500 people, 90 percent of them women, steadily sew jeans headed for the United States. In Velcas, the only Nicaraguan-owned factory in the Free Trade Zone, workers make jeans which the factory owner sells for $1.60 per pair. When they finally rest on the shelves of J. C. Penney, Wal-Mart, Sears and other stores, they will cost $15.95.

The owner of the factory claims that she is open to the formation of unions in her factory, but workers tell a different story. Throughout the Free Trade Zone workers report suppression of unions and labor organizing by both factory owners and the Nicaraguan government. This in spite of the numerous reasons in support of unionization. Exits in the Velcas factory are locked. Employees complain of forced overtime, lack of benefits and job security, 12-hour days, and inadequate wages—referred to by the workers as a "hunger salary." [6]

Abusive child labor is also widespread. The International Labor Organization estimated that in 1996 at least 120 million children between the ages of 5 and 14 worked full-time rolling cigarettes by hand, stitching soccer balls, knotting carpets and performing other labor-intensive tasks. [7] Too often, these children labor for long hours for little and sometimes no pay in unsafe and unsanitary working conditions. Their status resembles indentured servanthood.

Such abuse of basic labor rights is a matter of fundamental moral concern. One of the Ten Commandments, "Remember the Sabbath day, and keep it holy," is partly a protection against labor abuse. Family, servants, immigrants and even animals were to be given a day of rest (Dt 5:12–15).

How can such abuses be curtailed?

One way is to build labor rights, along with basic environmental provisions, into international trade agreements. Industries in developing countries shouldn't be required to pay wages that would be acceptable in industrial countries. That would eliminate the main advantage developing countries have in international competition. But countries that want to be part of the global economy should protect labor against slavery and child abuse and allow workers to organize.

Should trade agreements include provisions specifically related to hunger?

If a trade agreement is likely to make some people go hungry, compensatory steps should be required. For example, when the nations of the world agreed to freer trade in agriculture in 1994, they knew that sub-Saharan Africa would be hurt. African nations depend on food aid and had long benefited from special arrangements to sell their agricultural products in Europe. It was clear that more liberal trade in agriculture would reduce these benefits and cost poor people in Africa billions of dollars. The United States and the other nations agreed to compensate poor countries in Africa and elsewhere that would be hurt, but so far these countries haven't received any of the promised compensation.[8]

U.S. citizens who care about hungry people in Africa should insist that this agreement be respected, but Bread for the World finds it hard to organize people around such issues. Relatively few U.S. citizens pay much attention to international trade agreements and hardly anyone thinks about them from the perspective of hungry people. The authors have included a hefty section on global economics in this book, so that concerned citizens can begin to tackle issues like trade. It may seem a dull and difficult topic, but for people who are desperate for a place at the table, better trade policies may give them access.

Chapter 18

International Investment and Debt

We in Africa have many friends in the United States who have stood by us in the dark days of oppression and injustice. Many of our brothers and sisters of faith understand that Christianity is political or it is not Christianity.

Bread for the World is such a friend. For 25 years, Bread for the World has sought justice for vulnerable people, working to end hunger in Africa, in the United States and around the world. Now, the voices of a movement 44,000 members strong will join in a global movement of jubilee.

Developing countries in Africa, Latin America and Asia stagger under the increasing burden of international debt. In Tanzania, where 40 percent of the population dies before age 35, the government spends nine times more on foreign debt payments than on health care. Many who already struggle with hunger and poverty are further imprisoned by their countries' crippling debt.

But there is a way out. The biblical principle of jubilee reminds us that all belongs to God. In the jubilee year, debts are forgiven. Debtors make a new beginning. Countries burdened by unpayable debt deserve a new beginning. Children deserve to be free from malnutrition, to have basic health care, to have a chance at education. Their shoulders cannot and should not carry their country's burdens of debt.

Bread for the World is asking the U.S. Congress to help relieve the debt burden of the poorest countries, ensuring that the benefits reach people in need in those countries.

We need your support. We need your voice. So I ask you to Proclaim Jubilee: Break the Chains of Debt!

Archbishop Desmond Tutu[1]

Some developing countries are burdened with unpayable debts from the past. Bread for the World is campaigning to get some of the debt of the world's poorest countries canceled, and to make sure that it's done in a way that helps poor people. But the problem of unpayable debt should be seen in the larger context of international investment, which gives an important boost to economic progress in developing countries.

How important is international investment?

While the great bulk of the investment in most countries comes from *local* savings and entrepreneurship, foreign investment can also contribute to a country's economy. Commercial bank lending to developing countries increased dramatically in the 1970s and then abruptly plunged with the international debt crisis of the 1980s. In the 1990s, foreign investment in developing countries soared again. This time, foreign investors more often opened their own plants (foreign *direct* investment) or bought stock in local companies.

In 1990, $42 billion went to developing countries in net private foreign investment. By 1997 that number had jumped to $256 billion, including $162 billion in direct investment and stocks. This boom came to an end in the East Asian financial crisis of 1997.[2]

Virtually all developing countries, even North Korea, are eager for foreign investment. They need the money, and direct foreign investment can also bring technology and management skills. But about 80 percent of private financial flows to developing countries in the first half of the 1990s went to just 12 countries.[3] Bermuda received more foreign investment than India, although India has *18 thousand* times as many people.[4]

How can countries attract foreign investment?

When companies are deciding where to invest, they seek an investment climate that includes political stability and good economic prospects; reliable systems of transportation and communication; a low level of corruption; and a government that does not impose high taxes, regulations and bureaucratic delays. Investors are also looking for an educated, hard-working labor force at relatively low wages. They usually prefer lax labor laws and few environmental restrictions.

Any society would want some, but not all, of these things for itself. In deciding how to handle foreign investment opportunities, governments must balance economic, social and environmental goals.

Why did international investors suddenly retreat from East Asia in 1997, and what was the result?

A sustained economic boom, cronyism and inadequate regulation led some East Asian banks and businesses to overextend themselves. Some of them were heavily indebted to foreign creditors, and a wave of devaluations made those loans unpayable. As international investors raced to get out, a crisis deepened and spread. International investors even pulled back from countries as far away as Russia and Brazil, and the financial crisis became global.

The human impact was appalling. Before the crisis, it was estimated that 20 million Indonesians lived below the poverty line of one dollar a day. According to a World Bank estimate, that number doubled within the first months of the crisis. In Indonesia, Thailand and South Korea, school dropout rates soared, especially for girls. Families could no longer pay for education, and children needed to work for their family's survival. A study found that the number of street children in one major Indonesian city increased 43 percent in the months following the crisis, with 30 percent of the street girls depending on prostitution to support themselves.

This study, by *New York Times* correspondent Nicholas Kristof, further reported how the downturn hit Samrong Harwiset's family in northeast Thailand:

"My daughter and son-in-law are working in Bangkok, and so I'm look-ing after the five grandchildren on my own," Mrs. Samrong explained as she sat on a mat inside the home. "Then with the crisis, my daughter stopped sending money."

To get by, Mrs. Samrong and her grandchildren collect herbs in the mountains to sell. But that is not enough to cover expenses, so when a trader came by and offered $40 cash for her fifteen-year-old granddaugh-ter, Mrs. Samrong agreed. . . .

Mrs. Samrong says that the trader told her that the girl would work

*as a maid in Bangkok, but other girls had been sold into brothels before
in the village and the neighbors doubt that Mrs. Samrong was so naive.*

*Asked about that, Mrs. Samrong shrugged her shoulders ambigu-
ously. "When you're poor," she said, "you believe anything." . . .*

*So that is how Mrs. Samrong's granddaughter, Lamphan Ngao-
phumin, . . . came to be sold to a trader and eventually resold to a buyer
in Bangkok.*[5]

What can be done to keep financial crises like this from happening again?

Business interests and governments are looking for new ways to
promote and stabilize international investment. Industrial-
country governments have proposed a Multilateral Agreement
on Investment that would bind participating governments to
policies that facilitate international investment. Governments are
giving the International Monetary Fund (IMF) authority to over-
see how borrowing governments regulate international investment. In the wake of the financial crisis of 1997, officials and
academics talked about additional measures to make international investment less volatile.

Reducing the risks of financial crisis would be good for
people around the world, certainly for poor people in developing
countries. But so far, public interest groups and sometimes
developing-country governments have been on the margins of
negotiations about the rules for international investment.
Advocates for impoverished people should be pushing to open
these discussions and make sure that the interests of poor people
get considered.

Another problem with foreign investment is the backlog of
unpayable debt that many poor countries carry. Some countries
are still struggling with huge debts they acquired decades ago.

How big are the debts? And how did countries come to borrow more than they could afford to pay?

Developing countries owe more than two trillion dollars worldwide. Most of this is owed by middle-income developing countries. But over $500 billion of the debt is owed by low-income
developing countries.[6]

Sub-Saharan Africa pays more than $12 billion in debt service annually, and owes about eight billion dollars more that it cannot pay. About 10 percent of that total could provide the extra educational resources needed each year to give all the region's children a place in school.[7]

Take the case of Mozambique, which has the most serious debt load in Africa. In 1994, its total national debt was four and a half times its gross national product. How did Mozambique get caught in this trap? In 1975 it got its independence from Portugal, which had done almost nothing to educate Mozambique's people or prepare them for leadership. Mozambique soon became embroiled in a devastating internal conflict that lasted for more than a decade, fueled by the Cold War and the apartheid struggle in neighboring South Africa. The government was experimenting with Marxism, which seemed to some of Mozambique's leaders a better idea than the capitalism that Portugal had imposed. During this period the government borrowed heavily to fight terrorist rebels and keep a threadbare economy going. The government abandoned Marxism during the 1980s and negotiated a peace with the rebels in 1992, but the task of rebuilding a shattered economy has been painfully difficult—made all the more so because of that enormous burden of debt. Mozambique's case is unusual in some respects, but what is not unusual is that outside pressures had a lot to do with the origins of its debt.

What are the origins of developing-country debts?

Developing nations' debt originated for many reasons. Much of it represents prudent investments, just as the mortgage on your home, or a business or educational loan may be a good investment. When countries borrow money to fund productive projects, they are usually able to repay.

Developing countries have also borrowed money for projects that did more harm than good. In some cases, politicians were more concerned about immediate appearances (a fancy airport, for example) than long-term returns. In some cases, industrial countries offered loans to buy arms or other exports. In a few cases, corrupt tyrants, like the late President Mobutu of the Congo (then called Zaire), pocketed vast sums from aid and investment dollars while their countries slipped into economic chaos. The

United States and its allies let Mobutu get away with it because he was anticommunist.

But the overarching factor that led to a debt crisis for virtually all developing countries was a malfunctioning of the global economy.

What malfunction of the global economy?

It started in October 1973, as the oil exporting countries (OPEC) imposed an oil embargo on the West. The price of oil jumped from three dollars a barrel to $34 a barrel by 1981. Soaring oil prices burdened oil-importing developing countries with staggering new costs, while the oil-exporting countries suddenly had billions, then hundreds of billions of additional dollars to invest abroad. Much of it went to banks in the United States and other rich countries. The banks in turn needed borrowers for that money. What better way to solve everyone's problem than to recycle the petro-dollars through the banks to the developing countries, enabling them to pay for oil imports? So the bankers, along with the governments of the OPEC and the industrial nations, urged developing countries to borrow.

The oil crisis and deficit spending by the United States and other industrial countries led to higher and higher inflation. In the late 1970s, the U.S. Federal Reserve Board decided to strangle inflation by limiting the supply of money. This threw the global economy into a long and deep recession. Real interest rates soared to their highest level in 200 years. In 1982, 53,000 U.S. businesses went bankrupt. Because of high interest rates and low farm prices, thousands of U.S. farmers found themselves hopelessly in debt. The prices of most developing-country exports plummeted. When Mexico announced that it couldn't pay its debts, commercial banks around the world panicked. They withdrew credit from Mexico and other developing countries as well. The banks' sudden retreat added to the financial crisis in developing nations.[8]

Nearly all developing countries suffered a huge economic setback. Within a few years, the strongest and most adaptable developing economies had adjusted and were moving forward again. But many of the world's poorest countries are still saddled with huge, unpayable debts.

Why don't they just declare bankruptcy and start over with a clean slate?

The world doesn't have any orderly bankruptcy procedure for nations. By contrast, if a business or individual is hopelessly in debt, a judge establishes a debt-reduction plan. Lenders have to settle for partial repayment. The judge makes sure that all creditors lose proportionally. If the individual can't pay anything, the judge declares complete bankruptcy; the individual can no longer be hounded by creditors, but will find it difficult to borrow again.

If a person goes bankrupt, it takes years to rebuild his or her credit rating. But what developing countries face is far worse. All their creditors are demanding repayment, even though everyone knows this is impossible. There is no international equivalent to a bankruptcy court.

If a developing country says it won't pay its debts, nobody will do business with it. No more investment comes in, and banks won't help facilitate international trade. In today's world, if a country wants to get ahead, it better try to take advantage of opportunities in the global economy. In short, heavily indebted poor countries are caught in a debt trap.

What is the *human* cost of meeting those debt obligations?

High unemployment, depressed incomes, fewer children in school, no money to import medicines. In sum, what results is development in reverse: increasing poverty and more hunger.

A sad fact is that those who suffer the most had no part in incurring the debt. Janet Green, a development educator who serves on Bread for the World's board of directors, put it this way:

> I once compared a country's debt problem to a person's credit card debt. I was corrected. It was more like someone no longer in the picture had stolen that person's credit card and run up a lot of debt for which the owner was still responsible, but had none of the things that had been purchased.

What can be done to deal with the debt crisis?

A series of initiatives have helped countries cope with debt. In the late 1980s, Bread for the World helped convince Congress to authorize the cancellation of about three billion dollars in unpayable debt owed to the United States. In 1997, Bread for the World worked with Oxfam and others to shape and support an agreement that the World Bank and IMF would, for the first time, write off some of the debt that low-income, highly indebted countries owe them.

But many very poor countries are still burdened with unpayable and oppressive debts.

Pope John Paul II, Archbishop Desmond Tutu and many other church leaders have urged the forgiveness of oppressive poor-country debt as part of the world's celebration of the millennium. They cited the Old Testament year of jubilee. If people had fallen so far into debt that they lost their patrimonial land or became indentured servants to their creditors, freedom and land were to be restored once every 50 years in the year of jubilee.

Churches and other people of good will have joined together in a Jubilee 2000 campaign. As part of this campaign, Bread for the World is urging Congress to help reduce the debt of the world's poorest countries and to do so in a way that channels the benefits to poor people in those countries. Bread for the World's 1999 Offering of Letters is called *Proclaim Jubilee: Break the Chains of Debt.*

Why should the United States do anything to bail these countries out?

Unpayable debt doesn't help anybody, and an orderly cancellation will allow debtor countries to attract new investment and become contributors to the global economy. The more fundamental reason to reduce the debts of poor countries is moral and religious: financial obligations should be respected, but human needs take priority. Exodus 22 says that a creditor can't take a debtor's coat as a loan guarantee because the debtor will get cold. Deuteronomy 24:6 says a creditor can't take a millstone as a guarantee because the poor family needs the millstone to make bread.

The principle is clear: as important as financial obligations are, the basic needs of people take precedence.

A once-only cancellation of debts for some of the world's poorest countries could make the year 2000 a year of grace.

Chapter 19

Crumbs from the Table

Fourteen days before he died, President Kennedy spoke to a group of church leaders about foreign aid. He deplored the fact that it had dropped to a mere 4 percent of the national budget and added, "I do not want it said of us what T. S. Eliot said of others some years ago:

'Here were decent godless people;
Their only monument the asphalt road
And a thousand lost golf balls.'"[1]

Since that speech, U.S. foreign aid has dropped from 4 percent to less than 1 percent of federal spending.

U.S. citizens like to think of the United States as a generous nation. It rebuilt Europe after World War II. It sends foreign aid money all over the world. It provides grain to Africa and Asia in times of famine. But in fact the United States ranks *last* when compared to the 20 other industrialized donor countries in terms of the proportion of its national income given in aid to developing nations. Moreover, most U.S. foreign aid serves strategic or military goals rather than humanitarian or development goals.

Almost all the financial support the U.S. government gives to international efforts to reduce hunger and poverty comes from the foreign aid budget. That includes work on many of the matters discussed in this book—child survival, environmentally sustainable development, population, private sector development, health, education, women-in-development and debt reduction.

Yet Christians in this country have been almost totally silent while U.S. aid to poor countries has been shrinking. In 1996 alone, U.S. development aid to sub-Saharan Africa, where per capita food production and income have been declining for three decades, fell by 25 percent, with hardly a peep from the churches.

Perhaps the response of Christians would be different if they knew the facts. When a 1995 University of Maryland poll asked how much of the federal budget goes to foreign aid, the

Pulling Our Weight?
Official Development Assistance as % of National Income in 1997

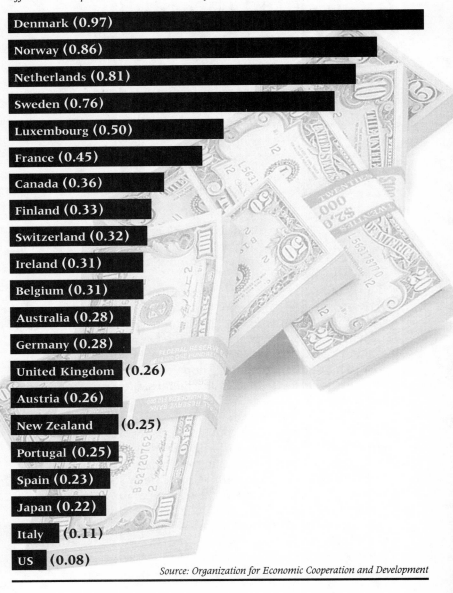

Denmark **(0.97)**

Norway **(0.86)**

Netherlands **(0.81)**

Sweden **(0.76)**

Luxembourg **(0.50)**

France **(0.45)**

Canada **(0.36)**

Finland **(0.33)**

Switzerland **(0.32)**

Ireland **(0.31)**

Belgium **(0.31)**

Australia **(0.28)**

Germany **(0.28)**

United Kingdom **(0.26)**

Austria **(0.26)**

New Zealand **(0.25)**

Portugal **(0.25)**

Spain **(0.23)**

Japan **(0.22)**

Italy **(0.11)**

US **(0.08)**

Source: Organization for Economic Cooperation and Development

respondents' average estimate was 15 percent. When asked what share of U.S. tax dollars *should* aid poor countries, respondents supported an average of 5 percent of federal spending. In fact, foreign aid spending is less than *1 percent* of the U.S. budget.[2]

Why has Congress been cutting development assistance?

The many reasons include:
- the need for fiscal restraint;
- a mistaken belief that the United States already spends too much on foreign aid;
- the end of the Cold War, which motivated many to support foreign aid;
- the belief that foreign aid is a failure, a waste of money;
- wariness about corruption in the recipient countries;
- a suspicion of anything the government does;
- the fact that most people in the United States sense little connection with people in the poorest countries;
- a lack of understanding about how foreign aid benefits our nation; and
- a lack of political leadership on this issue.

Why did the end of the Cold War reduce support for development aid?

Curbing the spread of communism was the major reason for U.S. aid from its inception after World War II, though it was closely tied to public support for helping desperate Europeans. For decades, governments that stood militantly against communism—and often against social reforms, as well—were lavished with aid, while neutral countries such as India got comparatively little. When communism collapsed, one of the main reasons for foreign aid disappeared.

The silver lining in that cloud is that foreign aid funds are now better focused on development and humanitarian needs. The U.S. Agency for International Development (USAID) and other international aid agencies now direct more of their aid to countries that are committed to sustainable development; and the aid agencies have increased their focus on poor people and grassroots development.

What lies behind the widespread public view that foreign aid is a big waste?

First, its use as a Cold War weapon led to much abuse. Second, helping countries out of poverty was a new initiative, and many mistakes were made. Consequently there were—and are—plenty of horror stories about bureaucratic schemes that didn't work, plans that failed because the people who were supposed to be helped had no part in designing and implementing them, food rotting on the docks, inappropriate technology, theft, corruption and much more. Such reports nourished critics on both the left and the right.

Betty Voskuil, head of the Reformed Church in America's hunger program, saw firsthand the worst and the best of foreign aid on a visit to the West African nation of Mali.

One day while driving through the countryside with a friend, we came across a huge concrete structure in the middle of a barren field. It was unclear what it was, simply because it seemed so out of place. We eventually came to believe that it was a dam, in spite of the fact that there was no water around it and no people staffing it. It was abandoned. All the money that had been poured into it was now serving no purpose.

Later in the trip we were again driving along and my guide pointed out an IFAD project to me. IFAD, the International Fund for Agricultural Development, is a branch of the United Nations devoted to the empowerment of poor, rural people around the world. The IFAD project consisted of little more than a couple of fields and some men plowing them with oxen and a single plow. But it appeared to be successful.

It was the juxtaposition of these two images that has remained most powerfully with me. One, the dam, represented a certain kind of international development which bypasses poor and hungry people. Someone had procured the necessary capital to build it, but it now languished in the dust. No one, least of all poor people, were benefiting from it. It appeared simply to be a million-dollar monument to poorly directed resources.

The IFAD agricultural project on the other hand stood for something much different. While not as immediately impressive, it was touching the lives of hungry people and empowering them in a tangible way. The dam wasn't feeding people; the single plow was. This is not to say that dams aren't important. Of course they are. It just reinforced for me the importance of development that does not bypass poor and hungry people. I was proud that Bread for the World had played a key role in getting Congress to support IFAD.

What's the best way to ensure that foreign aid programs really aid poor people?

Bread for the World has devoted much of its efforts over the years to supporting aid programs that work well for poor and hungry people as well as critiquing programs that should be reformed or, in some cases, eliminated.

Most foreign aid programs don't even claim to help poor people; the constituencies for other elements in the aid budget have more clout than the constituencies that defend development aid. For years, Bread for the World pushed to reduce military aid, and most military aid now goes to Israel and Egypt. A third of the aid budget goes to those two countries; its purposes are to protect Israel and maintain peace in the Middle East. The aid budget also includes programs that are intended mainly to help U.S. businesses overseas.

About half of the foreign aid budget goes to development and humanitarian purposes, but not all of that is focused on poverty reduction. About a third of the aid budget goes to humanitarian relief or focused efforts to overcome poverty or protect the environment.[3] Bread for the World works to protect and expand that third, especially through programs that help hungry and poor people improve their ability to help themselves. It has also urged aid agencies to promote grassroots participation in the projects they support. If poor people take part in decisions, they can make sure that money is spent well and meets their needs.

When Art Simon visited tribal villages near Calcutta, villagers proudly showed him a large reservoir they had dug with hand tools as part of a project that gave them food in exchange for their labor. This food-for-work project was administered by a church-sponsored agency, and the food came from USAID. Digging that reservoir and bringing barren land into production was a way of getting out from under the local moneylender—who had tried to keep the villagers from digging the reservoir by promising them water. When Simon asked them how much interest the moneylenders charged, the villagers cited bags of rice and days of labor, which translated into annual interest rates ranging from 200 to 300 percent. The reservoir allowed them to improve their nutrition, increase their incomes and develop economic leverage. By planning and building it together, they were also developing the community's capacity to get things done.

Government-supported aid agencies have gradually learned to work more at the grass roots, often by supporting private nonprofit groups. On the other hand, some key aspects of development necessarily happen at the macro level—a government's policies toward international trade and investment, for example. Fortunately, the spread of democracy and the increasing strength of grassroots groups worldwide have made popular participation in national policy decisions more feasible in many countries. Government-supported aid agencies can encourage this.

Will countries that receive foreign aid need it forever?

Portugal, South Korea and Taiwan used to receive aid but are now aid donors. Other countries, such as Thailand and Brazil, no longer receive aid but do get loans from government-supported agencies. They pay commercial interest rates but need some backing to borrow overseas for purposes such as schools or roads.

Poorer developing countries, such as Guatemala and Tanzania, still need outright aid. Levels of education and workforce skills are low. Health services and transportation are poor. Water and power supplies are often inadequate. Exports are meager. Because of such shortcomings, the poorest countries receive little private investment. All 47 countries of sub-Sahara Africa combined, excluding South Africa, received less than 1 percent of private capital flows in 1997.[4]

Won't some countries waste whatever aid they get?

Some countries are plagued with corruption, bad management and policies that obstruct development. For these nations, aid may do little or no good unless it goes directly to nongovernmental organizations that work in local communities. Government-supported aid agencies should and now do usually direct their aid to poor countries that are making good-faith efforts.

Aid to Uganda, for example, has made possible one of the most remarkable recoveries in Africa. Once known as "the pearl of Africa," Uganda suffered years of decline under brutal dictatorships and became one of the most impoverished countries in the world. In 1986, Yoweri Museveni seized power and began restoring the rule of law. He instituted difficult economic reforms, and Uganda's economy grew at an average annual rate of 6.7 percent for the next 12 years. It has also doubled or tripled its production of major crops.[5] Because its economy had sunk so low, Uganda remains a very poor country with a per capita income in 1996 of $300 a year. Foreign aid and IMF loans together fund almost half of the government of Uganda's annual $1 billion budget.

Like Uganda, many poor countries in Africa and elsewhere are reforming their economies and becoming more democratic. Aid gives these countries a much better chance to make progress against hunger.

What role do U.N. agencies play in aid to poor countries?

The U.N. Development Program is in the forefront of promoting sustainable antipoverty development efforts. The World Food Program coordinates emergency food aid. UNICEF has championed a revolution in child survival. The World Health Organization provides leadership on health issues. As Betty Voskuil witnessed in Mali, IFAD helps small-scale farmers become more productive and rural entrepreneurs to get businesses started. The list goes on.

One major advantage of working through U.N. agencies is that each dollar contributed by the United States is matched by many dollars from other countries. Despite the essential role of these agencies, the United States has become more than a billion dollars delinquent in its dues to the United Nations itself; and funding for U.N. agencies is a constant struggle in the U.S. Congress. U.S. influence has suffered as a consequence.

Does U.S. foreign aid benefit the United States?

The United States has a self-interest stake in development assistance:

- There's no way to protect the global environment without also helping hungry and poor people in the developing countries earn a decent living in an environmentally sustainable way.
- Desperation in Mexico, Central America and countries much farther away will also push people—welcome or not—to immigrate to the United States.
- The border patrol cannot stop the spread of diseases. AIDS and other diseases, some of them new and virulent, move rapidly from one country to another. Just as rich people in a community favor public health measures for their own protection, rich nations have a stake in health worldwide.
- Hunger, poverty and injustice contribute to violence. The United States often gets involved in relief efforts and sometimes in military intervention. Prevention is much cheaper than responding to crises.
- The world is now knit together in a global economy. If poor people around the world become more productive, the goods we buy from them will be cheaper and better. Those who have retirement money invested in mutual funds will get higher returns. When the incomes of poor people around the world rise, their imports from the United States rise. Conversely, if their economies falter, ours is also hurt.

Young people have a special stake in solving global problems. The older generation may suffer less from the impact of neglecting poverty, disease and environmental degradation in developing countries. But neglect now is sure to boomerang on people in the rich nations in years to come. For this reason, among others, students should be in the forefront of the antihunger movement.

But enlightened self-interest is still self-interest. God's gracious love for all the world's people and their great need are still the best reasons to help struggling people in developing countries. "God so loved the world . . ." and so should we. Christians cannot in good faith separate John 3:16–17 from 1 John 3:16–17: "We know love by this, that he laid down his life for us—and we ought to lay down our lives for one another. How does God's love abide in anyone who has the world's goods and sees a brother or sister in need and yet refuses to help?"

Chapter 20
The World Bank and the IMF

People here [in Bogor, Indonesia] are waiting to see which will go first, the chickens or the eggs. Either way, both foods may soon disappear from people's diets, heralding severe food shortages in the world's fourth most populous nation.

"We have almost no chickens left," said Ho Cu Ciong, who farms eggs here in Indonesia's poultry-breeding capital, 40 miles south of Jakarta. Already he has slaughtered or sold off most of his 90,000 chickens because of the high cost of feeding them. His eggs have become an expensive luxury item.

"If you ask me which will be the first to go down, it is both of them," he said. "In the market the shelves are already empty, empty, empty."

With the cost of imported chicken feed more than doubling because of Indonesia's weakened currency, 90 percent of the country's poultry farmers have already gone out of business. . . .

—Seth Mydans
The New York Times,
3 April 1998[1]

What do chickens and eggs in Indonesia have to do with the World Bank or the IMF?

World Bank assistance played an important part in helping Indonesia's economy take off, chickens and all, in the 1970s and 1980s. And in 1997 and 1998 the International Monetary Fund (IMF) gave Indonesia huge emergency loans to help its government deal with a financial crisis. The IMF urged Indonesia to devalue its money in order to increase its exports and reduce imports. Suddenly, imported chicken feed cost more, disrupting the chicken and egg market. That's how close these two international financial giants intertwine with the lives of ordinary people.

Talk about global institutions seems abstract and remote to most Americans. It puts people to sleep. But people in developing countries get interested—even agitated—when the World Bank and IMF are mentioned. These and other global institutions are important to hundreds of millions of poor and hungry people.

What are the roles of the World Bank and the IMF, and how do they affect developing countries?

The World Bank provides more money in development aid to the poorest countries than any other agency, and the IMF is the main source of emergency credit for countries facing a financial crisis. In the process of providing assistance, the World Bank and the IMF also influence the development policies of borrowing nations.

While working for the World Bank for 15 years, David Beckmann saw the bank's limitations and failures. The Bank financed many large, expensive projects that didn't benefit poor people and, in some cases, dislocated local communities. But Beckmann also saw projects that benefited millions of low-income families. In LaPaz, Bolivia, for example, he worked on a World Bank slum improvement project that gave tens of thousands of low-income families title to their land, clean water and other basic services.

The World Bank and the IMF were established in 1944, near the end of World War II, to provide a stable international money system (IMF), to finance postwar reconstruction and, later, to aid development in poor countries (World Bank). The World Bank lent about $21.1 billion at market interest rates to middle-income developing countries in 1997. The World Bank also has an affiliate, the International Development Association (IDA), which extends credit almost interest free to the poorest developing countries. IDA lent about $7.5 billion in 1997.[2] Unlike the World Bank, the IMF does not fund development projects. It advises countries on monetary policy and lends them money in emergencies. The IMF attaches conditions to these loans as a way of making sure that the borrowing governments are taking steps to get their economies in better shape.

In response to the international debt crisis, in the 1980s the World Bank and IMF began to work more closely together. Like the IMF, the World Bank also began to lend money to governments in support of economy-wide reforms. The IMF began to focus more on long-term changes in a country's economic structures, like the shutting down of unproductive, subsidized industries. The set of policies that the World Bank and IMF together promoted to help developing countries recover financial stability and growth were called "structural adjustment."

What exactly is structural adjustment?

In exchange for new loans, the World Bank and the IMF have required nations to make economic changes, such as cut government payrolls, reduce spending, open markets to imports and privatize industries. The IMF often requires currency devaluations. These conditions are strong medicine for countries already in economic crisis, and poor people are least able to cope with the resulting austerity and disruption.

Nicaragua has one of the world's most severe debt burdens. According to Witness for Peace, a faith-based social justice organization, structural adjustment has included systematically reducing social programs, contributing to the following conditions:

- Spending on health has been cut in half since 1988, meaning that many Nicaraguans no longer have access to adequate care.
- Because of education cuts, teachers' salaries cover less than half of what it costs to live at the poverty line, and classrooms are often crowded with 60 to 70 students.
- Unemployment increased to alarming levels while subsidies for public utilities, transportation and food were eliminated.[3]

When an economy is sinking, painful adjustments *must* be made, but the World Bank and IMF analysts have typically focused on economic efficiency and growth, sometimes ignoring the consequences for poor and vulnerable groups.

In response to criticism, the World Bank has devoted increasing attention to the impact of adjustment programs on poor people. It now routinely urges governments to protect budgets for basic education and health, for example. The IMF is also putting a bit more emphasis on the poor. In 1998, when the government of Indonesia cut fuel subsidies in response to its financial crisis, the IMF urged that the subsidy continue for kerosene, the household fuel poor families tend to use.

What are the World Bank and IMF doing to forgive debts?

In late 1996 they launched a debt initiative for highly indebted poor countries, most of them in Africa. Bread for the World helped mobilize political support for this initiative.

Uganda was the first country to receive debt forgiveness. Anticipating a reduction in its debt payments, the government began providing free primary education for up to four children per family. Until then, only two children per family could go to school. Children flooded into schools, and in some rural areas attendance doubled or tripled. What good will that do? Visiting Bread for the World members saw delighted children's faces. More substantively, schooling raises productivity, income and gender equality. In Uganda four years of primary education for a future farmer raises crop production by an average of 7 percent.[4]

What changes are needed at the World Bank and the IMF to make them more effective instruments in the struggle against hunger and poverty?

David Beckmann's experience at the World Bank confirmed both the need for and the possibility of World Bank reform. Because the World Bank is accountable to national governments (especially rich-country governments, which get 60 percent of the votes in its board), it sometimes serves their interests rather than serving poor people. The best corrective for this is to open up decisions to popular debate in both the lending and the borrowing countries.

Beckmann's last assignment in the World Bank was to initiate an institution-wide process for learning how the World Bank could promote democratic participation in the large-scale projects and policy shifts it supports. A few years after Beckmann took his present post, Bread for the World Institute became active on this issue, working with grassroots groups around the world to promote continued World Bank reform.

In 1997, Bread for the World launched a campaign among its members in the United States to get the World Bank to promote participation by people at the grass roots in projects it finances. Poor people and others who will be directly affected by projects *should* be involved in planning and implementation. During Bread for the World's campaign, the World Bank adopted new project preparation guidelines that urge its staff to promote local participation in the planning of many projects. In addition, Congress instructed the U.S. representative on the World Bank's board to urge the bank to "systematically consult with local communities on the potential impact of loans as part of the normal lending process and expand the participation of affected peoples . . . on the design and implementation of policies and projects." The Bread for the World staff drafted and urged Congress to adopt this instruction.

The IMF is a much more closed operation than the World Bank, but the IMF is also taking steps toward greater transparency and public accountability. In 1998, conservative Republicans in Congress picked up this issue, which environmental groups and Bread for the World have been pushing for years. Congress insisted on greater IMF transparency as a condition for approving a U.S. contribution to the IMF.

What about other global economic institutions?

Governments often make and implement rules and policies for the global economy through international institutions such as the World Bank and the IMF. These institutions also transmit global standards and expectations about how individual governments should deal with economic issues.

The World Trade Organization, launched in 1995, is another important global institution; it promotes international trade and helps to deal with trade disputes. Global trade negotiations take place within the framework of an overarching trade agreement called the General Agreement on Tariffs and Trade (GATT). The Group of 8 is another key institution of the global economy. It is comprised of the heads of state of the eight largest national economies; they meet once a year to set directions for the global economy.

Bread for the World and its members used to focus primarily

on changing policies and programs of the U.S. government. But increasingly, we need to work with like-minded citizens of other countries to influence policies and programs of the World Bank, the IMF and other international institutions. This adds complexity, but it is a necessary step, because many decisions that make or break opportunities for the world's hungry and poor people are made within global institutions.

The Politics
of
Hunger

Chapter 21

Charity Is Not Enough

Wanda has been coming to the agency on and off for about four years. This morning she had just received some fresh milk and pastries because she didn't have any money left to feed her two little girls breakfast. "It was a blessing because it's good food; the people are very nice and give you what you need, and they have things that kids like," says Wanda. "My husband works but at the end of the month we just run out of money. I wouldn't know what to do if I didn't have Christopher House."[1]

This snapshot of Christopher House in Chicago illustrates the vital role that charities play. This woman's family needs food today, not a debate about international economics. People who care about hunger must respond directly—by helping a family in need, volunteering at a community agency or supporting private agencies that assist poor people in other countries.

But effective help for hungry people walks on two legs—the leg of charity and the leg of public policy. People of good will must respond to immediate needs with immediate help; but the fight against hunger won't move forward if they don't also use the other leg and advocate better government policies.

How much are charities doing?

They are making a massive effort to deal with hunger and other human needs. In 1996, charitable organizations spent about $50 billion on human service programs in the United States, according to the Urban Institute's National Center for Charitable Statistics.[2]

Second Harvest is an umbrella organization for most of the nation's food banks. Its 186 local banks collect, store and distribute food and grocery products to almost 50 thousand local charitable organizations. The Second Harvest network includes almost a million volunteers and staff. In 1997, they provided emergency food assistance to 21 million people.

In the 1970s, there were only a scattering of emergency feeding agencies, mostly soup kitchens in low-income urban areas. But a whole generation has grown up thinking that it's normal for lots of people to get groceries at a local church.

It sounds like food banks are doing an impressive job. Isn't that enough?

First, the scale of response, though impressive, is small compared to the need. A Second Harvest study found that 29 percent of those obtaining emergency food assistance have to skip meals—some occasionally, some frequently—for lack of food and money. It also found that 45 percent of assistance programs run short of supplies. Even though almost all such programs limit the frequency of assistance, some still had to turn away clients.[3] One reason the food industry contributes to the Second Harvest network is that it has surplus or damaged products to give away; but the industry has found ways of reducing such losses. As a result, food banks haven't been able to expand much in recent years, even though the demand for emergency food has risen sharply.

Congress *cut* $28 billion from the food stamps program as part of the welfare bill of 1996. That's enough groceries to fill a convoy of army trucks that would stretch to the moon and back and then wrap around the earth four and a half times.[4] There's no way that charities can fill that gap.

If the nation's religious congregations tried to cover what the government now spends on food programs—as some policymakers have suggested—each of the estimated 350 thousand congregations in the country would have to raise an extra $110 thousand a year.[5] That's an *average*. Many of these congregations are quite small, including storefront and house churches with only a handful of members, and many others are located in low-income neighborhoods.

The Salvation Army warns: "Charitable programs must be seen as supplementary and complementary to government hunger programs. They cannot be a substitute. No private charity or consortium of private charities can supplant the government's role in addressing hunger . . . nor should they."[6]

Another problem is that kitchens and pantries are often located more for the proximity and convenience of the donors than for hungry clients. Most people prefer to support charities in their own communities, so charities tend to be stronger in wealthy communities, where donors live, than in poor communities. The two wealthiest city council districts in Manhattan have more soup kitchens than the two poorest.[7] The agencies of charity in poor rural areas tend to be weak and scattered. Indeed, the nation's charities are like a patchwork quilt with a lot of patches missing.

Most important, charities and governments have fundamentally different roles and capabilities. If churches, for example, tried to provide a complete safety net for the nation, they would have few resources for preaching the gospel, teaching individuals and families how to live and share, and ministering to personal needs in a caring way. On the other hand, churches and charities cannot do some of the most important things that government can do to reduce hunger—use the tax system to increase pay for low-income workers, for example, or maintain good public schools.

Janet Poppendieck, author of *Sweet Charity? Emergency Food and the End of Entitlement*,[8] argues that the spectacular growth of emergency feeding over the last two decades has inadvertently relieved pressure on the government to do its part. The result, she concludes, is more, not fewer, hungry Americans—not a conclusion the authors agree with; but she has pointed out a real danger: that unless direct assistance is accompanied by citizen advocacy, it plays into the hands of those who would divest the government of its responsibility for public justice.

A few years ago Bread for the World Institute surveyed 71 food banks in the Second Harvest network and found that only four had allocated 2 percent or more of their budgets for advocating better government policies or trying to stave off government cuts in food programs. Two-thirds (66 percent) of the food banks had no budget at all for such a purpose, though more than half said that they at least did some lobbying. Much of that is narrowly focused on matters that affect food bank supplies, however.[9] Food banks in the Second Harvest network and assistance groups related to them could become far more involved in advocacy. The reduction of hunger in the United States may in large part depend on the extent to which those in the emergency food network take on this additional challenge.

U.S. Foreign Aid
Private and Public

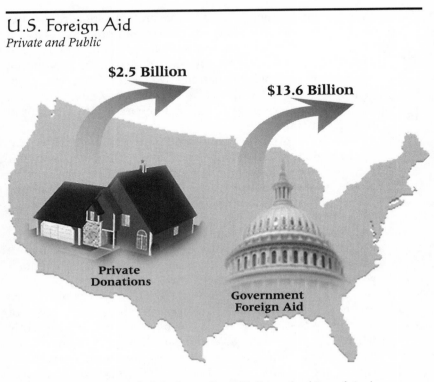

$2.5 Billion

$13.6 Billion

Private Donations

Government Foreign Aid

1995 data. Source: OECD, Development Cooperation, 1997; Congressional Research Service, CRS Report for Congress, 1998.

What are charities doing about *world* hunger?

Church-related agencies and other U.S. private voluntary organizations educate children and provide health care for needy families around the world. They assist with food, medicine, clothing and shelter in humanitarian emergencies. They improve the lives of many poor people by providing wells, seeds and tools, animals, small loans, skills training and much more. Private aid covers a wide range of activities related to emergency relief, social and economic development, care of the environment, democratic institutions, building up the capacity of community and civic groups, and advocacy for poor people, women and racial or ethnic minorities. The work is difficult and demanding, but for the most part private agencies do it exceedingly well.

U.S. private contributions through these agencies come to $2.5 billion a year. The U.S. government contributes another $0.7 billion a year through these agencies.[10]

Is it a good idea for the U.S. government to fund private aid agencies?

It's a way for private agencies to expand their grassroots work, and for the U.S. government to have its dollars used well. For example, Christian Children's Fund (CCF) began innovative work in Angola to help children deal with the scars of civil war. Most of the children in that country have experienced trauma from witnessing or suffering violence. CCF training teams travel from place to place, training teachers, community leaders and others. They help people learn from one another how to get children to deal with their experiences, so they can live constructively and not repeat the pattern of violence. The project was funded mainly by the U.S. Agency for International Development (USAID). While many private charitable efforts remain local in scope, USAID's global reach and financial resources led to the replication of this CCF project in other countries.

Sometimes government and private agencies work best when they work together. When child survival programs are administered by charities, the average benefits are higher than for commercial contractors or government health ministries. But USAID has developed and insists on high standards among the charities it helps fund. These have enhanced the performance of private aid agencies. In this instance, the U.S. government and private agencies contribute to each other's work. One plus one equals three.

Are most private agencies trustworthy or are some of them scandal ridden?

The vast majority are trustworthy and are making a substantial contribution to the betterment of people's lives. More than 150 private agencies in international development are part of an association called InterAction, and they have all subscribed to high standards of ethics and administration.

How can individual agencies be assessed? Reading their literature reveals what they are doing. Are they meeting urgent needs? Are they also working on long-term solutions to hunger and injustice?

Agencies sponsored by church denominations—such as Catholic Relief Services, Church World Service, Lutheran World Relief or the United Methodist Committee on Relief—have the advantage of a built-in constituency, which usually lowers their fundraising costs. They also have well-established accountability mechanisms, including a role for denominational leaders in supervising the agency's work. If you contribute to your own church's international assistance agency, your money will almost certainly be well used. Other well-established agencies, such as Oxfam, CARE and World Vision, also have strong accountability mechanisms.

Some people check on how much money an agency spends on programs in relation to fundraising and administration. But good administration is essential to effective work, and fundraising is also necessary. As a rule of thumb, both administration and fundraising should not consume more than 25 percent of an agency's budget.

The media have exposed some cases of abuse, but the media's vigilance is itself one assurance that most charities are responsible. If there is a scandal concerning these agencies, it lies in a different area, one that the media have not yet noticed.

A scandal? What is the scandal?

The scandal is taking a pass on advocacy. Most agencies are doing exemplary work in helping people. But most do little to influence U.S. public policy. Many of the grassroots leaders with whom U.S. charities work in developing countries have been pleading for more vigorous advocacy vis-à-vis the U.S. government and international agencies such as the World Bank.

Private agencies need to think more deeply about their mission. If an agency's mission is to help lift people out of hunger and poverty, then *not* engaging in advocacy is gross negligence, because the U.S. foreign aid budget is more than five times the combined contributions of private aid agencies to developing countries. And the government's influence on the rules of international trade and finance has an even bigger impact on poor people.

Catholic Relief Services, most agencies connected to Protestant denominations and several other private voluntary organizations have expanded their advocacy activities. Over the last ten years, InterAction has become an important advocacy voice with Congress and the administration on foreign aid issues. But advocacy still amounts to a tiny share of these agencies' combined $2.5 billion budget, and most of them seldom let their donors know how important U.S. government policies are or urge grassroots advocacy.

Private assistance agencies do magnificent work in relief and development. But if they would speak up more forcefully for the people they serve, the agencies could multiply their impact and make room for many more guests at the table.

Chapter 22

The Government
Has to Do Its Part

> The poor object to being governed badly, while the rich object
> to being governed at all. —*G. K. Chesterton*[1]

> [T]he powerful are more inclined to be generous than to grant
> social justice. —*Reinhold Niebuhr*[2]

Why should the government have a role in alleviating hunger?

A government role is essential because there are things that the
private sectors cannot or will not do. For this reason the government has a responsibility to guarantee public justice. Its role is
limited, and it should not try to do what can be done better by
other units of society.

Private enterprise and nonprofit groups have a wide-open
field when it comes to the problem of hunger. No one is holding
them back. They can do as much to reduce hunger as they have
the ability and desire to do. But experience has shown that
without an active government role, huge numbers of people get
trapped in hunger and poverty. If we are to end most hunger, or
even reduce it, there has to be a partnership, with each segment
of society doing what it can do best.

"Some argue that since individual Christians are com-
manded to care for the poor, it must not be any of the government's business," wrote Ron Sider and Fred Clark in *Christianity
Today*. "But such a conclusion requires that we dismiss the large
body of biblical teaching that says the government has a responsibility to care for the poor. It also ignores centuries of biblically
based Christian thought and teaching on the distinct but complementary roles of state, family and church."[3]

What are some things government can do better than the private sector?

Foreign policy is by definition the government's responsibility, and U.S. foreign policy has a great impact on hunger throughout the world. U.S. trade policies, for example, go a long way in determining employment opportunities for people on every continent. The nation's financial policies, the shape and size of its foreign aid and what it does or doesn't do in cooperation with other nations—all of these have a great bearing on whether or not millions of people have a place at the table.

And within the United States many decisions by the government affect poor people. Establishing and enforcing environmental standards affect them. So do policies regarding jobs, health, education, welfare and racial discrimination. The government has an obligation to ensure public justice.

What do you mean by public justice?

Public justice is solidly grounded, if not precisely defined, in the Bible. Consistent with the biblical witness, a government committed to public justice would seek for its people (1) their safety; (2) their civil rights, including rule of law and fairness in application of the law; (3) their opportunity to secure essential food, clothing, shelter, health care, education and employment; and (4) their freedom to live without government intrusion in matters that are better dealt with by the family, the church, private enterprise and voluntary associations. The U.S. Constitution spoke eloquently when it listed the purposes of our government:

> . . . to form a more perfect Union,
> establish justice,
> insure domestic tranquillity,
> provide for the common defense,
> promote the general welfare, and
> secure the blessings of liberty. . . .

That's a positive view of the government's role. People in the United States tend to be suspicious of government, especially the federal government, and that tendency has grown in recent years. Partly because of this suspicion, U.S. Christians are inclined to be privately generous and publicly stingy when it comes to hunger. Or perhaps they just don't want to bother with policy matters. The result is the same.

But haven't federal government programs to reduce hunger and poverty failed?

In 1996 government benefit programs, including Social Security and the Earned Income Tax Credit, cut poverty almost in half. The private economy by itself would have left more than 57 million people below the poverty line, but federal programs lifted 27 million of them out of poverty.[4] Federal assistance programs are far from perfection, but they make a huge difference.

If both government and other social units have essential roles, how do you determine who does what?

The purposes of various units of society (families, churches, schools, businesses, charities, neighborhood groups) are distinctive, and there is need for them to work in partnership. The principle of subsidiarity, prominent in Catholic social thought, says we should not do at a higher structural level what smaller and more local units (starting with the family) can do better. But, as Catholic thought has also emphasized, that does not mean a passive role for government. Through the government the whole society can work together on goals such as the reduction of hunger and poverty.

We can learn from experience. Orville Freeman, former U.S. secretary of agriculture, says that one of the keys to our success as a nation has been the marriage between private enterprise and the public sector. He cites the land-grant system that did so much for the development of U.S. agriculture. Land was offered to farmers, and states were given land for establishing land-grant colleges, as well as research and extension services. The seed salesman brought new technology to the farmer, while the extension system kept farmers informed and the salesman honest.

In 1932, the peak of the Great Depression, 25 percent of the work force was unemployed. Hunger and poverty were rampant. Our economy had clearly exposed flaws sufficiently deep that capitalism itself seemed in jeopardy, unable through any self-correction to get the economy growing again. So the government became innovative, setting up a new and more soundly insured banking system, for example, and stimulating the economy through federal spending on public works. The depression finally ended during World War II, when the entire nation mobilized to defend freedoms throughout the world. Government activism before and during the war played an essential part in lifting the nation out of the depression, giving free enterprise an enormous boost in the process. The fact that the nation was mobilized around a common cause had much to do with this success.

Social Security was an accomplishment of the government during the depression, one that proved to be a great boon to the entire nation. It may need fixing now, but few would call it a failure. Social Security and Medicare have lifted many elderly people out of poverty, making their lives longer and happier. That is an impressive accomplishment. The irony is that the children of our nation have taken the place of the elderly as the age group most entrenched in poverty—an indication of where corrective action is now most needed.

In these examples the government does not replace the efforts of other units of society, but enables them to function more effectively. The role of the government is to give others freedom and encouragement to do well what they are designed to do, while assuring a floor of justice for everyone. That requires a partnership of public and private efforts.

Isn't the U.S. government already spending a lot to help poor people?

According to a national survey conducted by *The Washington Post*, the Kaiser Foundation and Harvard University, 64 percent of the U.S. public thinks that foreign aid is one of the two largest areas of spending in the U.S. government budget. In fact, the U.S. government spends 0.8 percent of its budget on foreign aid. Twenty-six percent of the public believes that food stamps is one of the two largest areas of spending by the U.S. government. In the public's eye, only foreign aid and defense are more commonly seen as big areas of government spending. In fact, food stamps account for only a small percent of federal spending.[5]

Federal Budget
Fiscal Year 1997

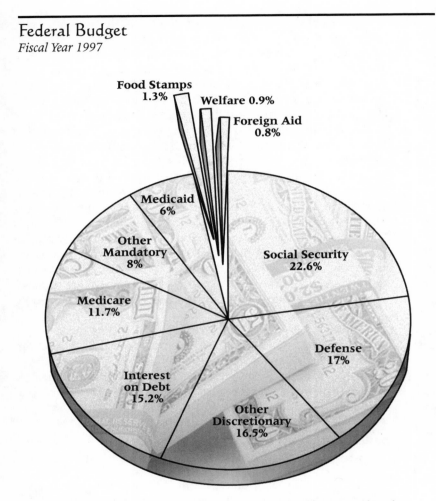

Food Stamps 1.3%

Welfare 0.9%

Foreign Aid 0.8%

Medicaid 6%

Other Mandatory 8%

Social Security 22.6%

Medicare 11.7%

Defense 17%

Interest on Debt 15.2%

Other Discretionary 16.5%

Foreign aid includes development aid, export programs, and security aid to Egypt and Israel.

The official name for welfare is Temporary Assistance for Needy Families (TANF). Includes child care and child support enforcement for TANF recipients.

Mandatory programs are automatically funded by previous law. They include programs such as veteran's pensions, federal retirement payments, and the Earned Income Tax Credit.

Discretionary programs' funding levels are determined each year by Congress. Includes programs such as NASA, Head Start, and transportation.

Source: OMB

The U.S. budget deficit has served politicians for two decades as a major excuse for cutting foreign aid and domestic anti-poverty programs. In 1996, Congress and the president clashed all year and finally shut down the U.S. government in a debate about how to reduce the deficit. In the end, the main cuts in spending on which they could agree were in foreign aid, welfare and food stamps! In 1998, the U.S. government ran a $70 billion surplus, but neither the president nor the leaders of Congress suggested a significant increase in spending to reduce poverty in the United States or worldwide.

If government has such a positive role, why is it subject to so much criticism?

Big bureaucracies are often clumsy and, like other institutions, need scrutiny to hold them accountable and compel reforms. But the constant barrage of rhetoric that depicts government as the cause of all our problems is destructive and has given the U.S. public an unduly dismal view of its government. In any case, revitalizing government depends on a revitalized citizenry. Citizens can rally around programs that work well, such as WIC, and change those that do not.

The word *idiot* is instructive. It comes from the Greek *idiotes*, which in ancient Greece referred to an ignorant person who did not participate in civic affairs. Maybe they were on to something. Maybe it is idiotic for citizens of the greatest democracy in the world to ignore public policy. If that is the secular judgment, the moral judgment may be that it is scandalous, surrendering as it does an opportunity to weigh in for people who struggle against the odds for enough food. And the religious judgment may be that it violates the grace of God, who welcomes all to the table.

Chapter 23
Guns and Bread

She straggled into the Government-held town of Wau yesterday on legs no thicker than broomsticks, a gaunt and skeletal figure with hollow eyes, her skin hanging loose over her bones.

She said she left three of her children under a tree a few miles back. They were too weak to go on after a four-day walk from Gogrial County to find food. Three other children had already died of starvation, she said.[1]

Scenes like these occur daily in famine-stricken Sudan, where a brutal civil war has been raging intermittently for decades. Perhaps the most fundamental purposes of governments are "to insure domestic tranquillity" and "provide for the common defense." But the government of Sudan and antigovernment rebels attack and sometimes deliberately starve populations in southern Sudan. It's an extreme example of armed conflict as a cause of hunger.

Excessive military spending is also a cause of hunger. President Dwight D. Eisenhower said starkly: "Every gun that is made, every warship launched, every rocket fired signifies, in the final sense, a theft from those who hunger and are not fed, those who are cold and are not clothed."[2]

How does conflict cause hunger?

It does so both directly and indirectly. One direct way is by using food as a weapon. Armies sometimes try to starve the enemy by destroying crops and blocking the delivery of emergency supplies, though the "enemy" is overwhelmingly women, children and other civilians. War also uproots millions of people who have to flee for their lives, forced to live in squalor with no way of feeding, clothing or sheltering themselves. More than 75 percent of the world's 50 million displaced persons are women and children.[3]

The Sudanese civil war has displaced millions of people, including 20 thousand "lost boys" who in 1990 traveled great distances to escape the violence, battling hunger, disease and fear along the way. They fled their homes and families also to escape the prospect of being forced to fight in the war themselves. Some of these boys survived weeks of harsh travel to reach Ethiopia. There they found temporary relief and safety. However, in 1991 the Ethiopian government changed hands, and the boys who had found refuge were forced to trek back to Sudan during severe and sometimes deadly rains. Simon Majok recounted the bitter memory of this refugee existence: "We were suffering because of war. Some have been killed. Some have died because of hunger and disease. We children of the Sudan, we were not lucky."[4]

And the indirect cause?

Indirectly, conflict causes hunger by devastating economies, destroying livelihoods, robbing children of education and impoverishing people. The U.N. Development Program reports that "many more people die from indirect causes—such as the disruption of food or water supplies or the destruction of health services"—than from lethal weapons.[5]

Land mines illustrate the indirect and lingering consequences of conflict. An estimated 110 million land mines are waiting to explode in 64 countries.[6] They are cheap and easy to deploy but the process of finding and dismantling them is slow, costly and dangerous. Because land mines also continue killing and maiming people long after a war has ended, a country such as Angola, which may have 10 million mines scattered about, faces a huge obstacle to making much of its farmland safe for farming.

The 30-year civil war in Angola drove more than two million Angolans from the countryside to seek safety in coastal cities. According to the World Bank, "The exodus of peasants to cities has drastically undermined Angola's rural economy, as well as urban conditions. Farmers who once made their living off the land now live in impoverished squatter settlements around cities such as Luanda. While fertile lands remain underused, urban unemployment further exacerbates poverty and crime."[7]

Doesn't hunger also contribute to conflict?

Hunger and the extreme poverty that typically goes with it are a destabilizing force. If they occur in the context of huge disparities between the rich and the poor, they may well provoke or nourish an armed revolt or other forms of violence. Impoverished people do not always suffer quietly. The uprising of the Zapatistas in the state of Chiapas, Mexico, illustrates this. So does the violence in many low-income U.S. neighborhoods.

A State Failure Task Force in the Central Intelligence Agency studied the causes of failed states.[8] It considered 600 possible factors in 113 cases of state failure (defined as revolutionary or ethnic wars, mass killings and disruptive regime changes). Then it selected 31 factors that most accurately explained success or failure and used combinations of these to create models for predicting state failure. The CIA found that *high infant mortality* was the single best predictor of state failure. They also learned:

- Democracy lowers the risk of state failure, while autocracy increases it. However, economically poor democracies are more unstable than poor nondemocracies, and if they don't improve living standards, these democracies are especially vulnerable.
- High levels of openness to trade seem to inoculate any type of regime against failure. Mass killings are frequently associated with low levels of openness to trade. (Countries with little foreign trade are of little concern to the international community, so mass killings are more apt to be tolerated, the study suggests.)
- Having a large share of young adults in the population increases the risk of ethnic war, because unemployed youth are more easily mobilized for such action.

Each of these factors is connected to hunger and poverty.

In what sense does military spending contribute to hunger?

The world spends about $700 billion a year for defense and military purposes.[9] Money allocated for arms and weapons is money that is not available for the kind of development that reduces hunger. In the United States, investment in a strong military is intended to strengthen security. This enormous expenditure ($280 billion in 1999) could be reduced if the nation strengthened its security in other ways, such as investing more in development assistance so that far more costly military interventions are less likely to be needed. Laura D'Andrea Tyson, former economic advisor to President Clinton, wrote during the Asian economic crisis, "We would spend billions of dollars to counter a destabilizing military threat in Asia. Surely we should be willing to pay a fraction of the cost to counter an economic crisis equally threatening to regional stability."[10]

Although U.S. and world military spending has declined sharply since the early 1980s, military expenditures are comparable to earlier Cold War levels despite the end of the Cold War. Lawrence J. Korb, assistant secretary of defense in the Reagan administration, points out that "the U.S. military is more than competitive. It already outspends all of its potential rivals combined and, together with its NATO allies, Japan, South Korea and Israel, accounts for 80 percent of the world's military expenditures." Korb notes that the nation is still spending $25 billion a year on strategic nuclear forces, including the building of new nuclear bombs; that it is planning to spend $500 billion "on three new tactical aircraft when its current planes are already the best in the world"; and that it still has a hundred thousand troops in Europe.[11] And in 1999, both the president and the Congress were committed to a rapid and sustained expansion of military spending.

Military leaders have a built-in disposition to ask for more than they need, because they must be prepared to cope with the worst possible contingencies. Members of Congress also continue to appropriate billions of dollars for weapons programs that the Pentagon does not even want, because they mean jobs in various congressional districts.

In developing countries, military allocations are also too high. What these countries spend is modest compared with the U.S. military budget, but they need those precious resources for education, agriculture and industry. Some countries are compelled to spend much. Guerrilla conflicts near the northern and western borders have forced Uganda to use one-fifth of its annual budget to defend the region, a painful but necessary

World Military Expenditures
billion dollars

Source: Michael Renner, "Military Expenditures Continue to Decline," In Lester R. Brown, Michael Renner and Christopher Flavin, Vital Signs 1998 (New York: W. W. Norton., 1998), 114–15. In 1995 dollars.

expenditure for this progressive East African nation. But in many cases heavy military spending simply reflects undue influence on the part of the military and the determination of authoritarian rulers to repress the dissent of their own citizens.

What can be done to encourage a shift of dollars from the military to development?

First, the public must be educated about the true cost of military spending, including lost opportunities for humane economic development.

Second, arms limitation agreements for weapons of mass destruction and for conventional arms must be encouraged.

India's testing of nuclear weapons only provoked Pakistan to do the same.

Third, arms sales to autocratic regimes must be stopped. In general, arms sales that may destabilize regions must be discouraged, especially sales by the United States, the world's largest arms merchant.

Finally, advocates for the hungry should share their views about military spending, especially by writing members of Congress.

Taking its inspiration from the words of Isaiah, "They shall beat their swords into plowshares," Bread for the World devoted its 1990 Offering of Letters to military spending and armed conflict. The Cold War was just coming to an end. Bread for the World's *Harvest of Peace* resolution called for a redirection of resources from the military to programs to meet human needs. Although Congress failed to adopt it, the resolution won extensive support in Congress and in a modest way helped set the stage for military spending reductions over the next several years.

In 1991, Bread for the World's Offering of Letters focused on violence in the Horn of Africa. War in Ethiopia, Somalia and Sudan was causing widespread death and starvation. U.S. policy in the region had long been driven by Cold War considerations, and both the U.S. and the U.S.S.R. had fueled violence and hunger. Bread for the World's proposed Horn of Africa Recovery and Food Security Act urged the United States to support peace, development and food security. The legislation gradually gained broad bipartisan support, but Representative Dante Fascell then tacked the bill onto the Foreign Assistance Authorization Bill, which was in trouble. Months passed with no progress on the bill. Finally, in March of 1992, one of Bread for the World's media activists, Peter England, contacted the *Miami Herald* in Fascell's home district, talked with the publisher and then with one of the *Herald*'s editorial writers, Ramon Mestre. Mestre made no commitment to do an editorial. England followed up his request with a letter. Thirteen days later the *Herald* ran an editorial that urged Fascell to cut the Horn of Africa bill loose from the foreign aid bill. Fascell did so that morning, and Bread for the World's Horn of Africa bill passed both houses by voice vote within the week. President George Bush signed the Horn of Africa Recovery and Food Security Act into law.

The legislation's strong congressional support had already encouraged the State Department to help negotiate an end to fighting in Ethiopia. This act has permitted development aid to Ethiopia and Somalia, despite the unpaid debts of prior regimes, and directed USAID to take a grassroots approach in its aid to Ethiopia.

"Never before have I been as awed by the incredible power an individual can wield in a democracy," England said of the great payoff for suffering and hungry people that resulted from his persistence.

God invites us to be peacemakers: "Blessed are the peacemakers, for they will be called children of God" (Mt 5:9), Jesus said. But those who make peace will also be helping to end hunger in God's world.

Chapter 24

Democracy and
Human Rights

> Perhaps the most dramatic measure [in Mali] was the cre-
> ation last year of a sort of annual national open forum. During
> the event, which lasts for several days in December and is
> broadcast live on national radio, the prime minister and mem-
> bers of government publicly answer the questions of citizens
> who come or write from all over the country.
>
> "This may have all started to please the outside world,"
> said Tore Rose, the resident representative of the United
> Nations Development Program, "but the important thing is
> that people have come to believe in their right to criticize and
> question their leaders, and that is a very powerful agent for
> change."
>
> —Howard W. French,
> *The New York Times*,
> 16 October 1996[1]

Mali is one of the poorest countries in Africa, but institut-
ing a democratic government has already made a vast amount of
difference in the lives of ordinary Malians. Just four years after
democracy was launched in 1992, Malian citizens told *New
York Times* reporter Howard French that their government "has
allowed them to make consensus decisions on the use of scarce
resources, helped them limit corruption and favored stability in
a region known for its coups."

French has also described conditions in Nigeria, where the
absence of democracy led to poverty in a resource-rich nation:

> Nigeria in the oil boom of the 1970s had the 33d highest per
> capita income in the world, but by last year, it slipped to the
> 13th poorest nation, according to United Nations figures. At

the same time, foreign diplomats and Nigerian critics of military rule say the top generals have siphoned off billions of dollars in oil revenue for personal profit.

In the late 1970s, the national currency, the naira, was worth twice as much as the dollar. Nowadays, it is worth about one cent. In business surveys, the country ranks as one of the most corrupt.[2]

Ultimately, hunger exists because of insufficient political will to address its causes. Creating the political will to address hunger is far more likely in a democratic society. In addition to encouraging participation from all levels of society, a democratic government is held accountable for its actions in every election cycle and is therefore more likely to respect its citizens' human rights.

What do you mean by "human rights"?

These include civil and political rights, but also social and economic rights such as clothing, shelter, medical care, education and food.

Is there an internationally recognized right to food?

The right to food is a good example of a social or economic right. It is included in the United Nations' Universal Declaration of Human Rights of 1948. In 1976, the U.S. Congress passed Right to Food resolutions at the prompting of Bread for the World. The resolutions began by restating a national commitment, set forth in the Declaration of Independence, that all people are endowed by their Creator with "the inalienable right to life, liberty, and the pursuit of happiness." None of these, the resolutions noted, "can be realized without food to adequately sustain and nourish life. . . ." Passage of the Right to Food resolutions was Bread for the World's first big legislative victory.

Ironically, the U.S. government has recently retreated from earlier affirmations of the right to food. At the World Food Summit of 1996, the administration refused to agree that food is a right.

How important are civil rights and democracy in the struggle against hunger?

Democratic countries almost never permit famines (see chapter 6). In contrast, Mao Zedong presided over what may have been the most disastrous famine in history. Mao's China made great strides against hunger by forcibly imposing social systems that lifted most people out of destitution. But an estimated 30 million people starved to death from 1959 to 1961 as a result of the Great Leap Forward, Mao's effort to rapidly develop heavy industry.

North Korea provides a more recent example.

A visit to [the] remote and desolate city [of Hamhung] near North Korea's eastern coast provides a rare glimpse of the country's near-total economic collapse. The crisis is over food—or the lack of it—but the country's problems run much deeper, to the core of a socialist system that has simply ceased to function. . . .

The [city's] orphanage is divided into several small rooms, with playpens for the smallest infants. Almost all of the children are malnourished, with browning hair, bald patches on their scalps and sores on their heads and faces. The most severely malnourished are listless and unresponsive. . . .

About 70 percent of the children here were orphaned when their parents died of malnutrition or disease. . . . The other 30 percent simply were abandoned and left for dead by parents too poor and too hungry to feed them.[3]

By some estimates, the extent of starvation in North Korea in the late 1990s was comparable to Ethiopia in 1984 and Somalia in 1992. But while Ethiopia and Somalia ultimately benefited from a stream of stark media images, North Korea's situation was exacerbated by closed borders, controlled information and a totalitarian dictatorship.

How do democracy and hunger interact in the United States?

This country is blessed with exceptionally strong and long-lasting democratic institutions that have made government and society more responsive to people's needs. But democracy has yet to

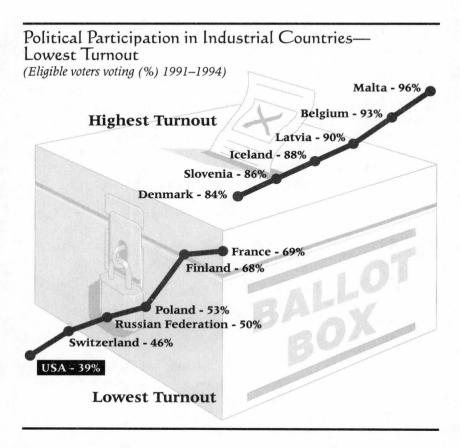

Political Participation in Industrial Countries— Lowest Turnout
(Eligible voters voting (%) 1991–1994)

Highest Turnout

Malta - 96%
Belgium - 93%
Latvia - 90%
Iceland - 88%
Slovenia - 86%
Denmark - 84%

France - 69%
Finland - 68%

Poland - 53%
Russian Federation - 50%
Switzerland - 46%

USA - 39%

Lowest Turnout

overcome extensive hunger here because too few citizens have demanded it.

U.S. voter participation is exceptionally low, and voter participation among low-income citizens is even lower than for the nation as a whole. Voters in general, but especially poor people, tend to be skeptical about making a difference in politics. But their withdrawal from politics forfeits power to special interests. That's regrettable, because Bread for the World has seen, again and again, that a few active citizens can have a disproportionate influence on government policies that affect hungry people. The use or neglect of one's influence as a citizen often determines whether or not others can join us at the table.

Chapter 25

Can We Afford to End Hunger?

> Dear Lord,
> give bread to the hungry,
> and hunger of Thee to those who have bread.
> —*An old Scottish prayer*

While the Bible is laced with promises of a day beyond history when no one will go hungry, some hunger seems inevitable in the world as we know it. Even if society did everything it could to help (which will not happen this side of our Lord's return), some individuals with fractured lives will go hungry. Despots and violence will continue to cause suffering, and economic fluctuations will occur. Yet eliminating the sort of routine, pervasive hunger the world now tolerates is feasible. This was already true 25 years ago, when Bread for the World began. It is even more clearly so today. Twenty-five more years of experience has shown that countries can, if they try, dramatically reduce hunger—or, out of neglect, allow hunger to spread. Experience has also demonstrated particular approaches that are effective and could be expanded.

But overcoming widespread hunger is such a daunting goal. Wouldn't it require massive changes?

The world has already made significant gains against hunger, mainly because of broad-based economic, social , environmental and political progress. The global economy continues to expand (albeit unevenly, and in spurts), and democracy and environmental concern have become more widespread over the last two decades.

173

Targeted efforts to reduce hunger and poverty are also being made, but the world has made less effort to overcome poverty than it has to achieve economic growth, democracy or even environmental protection. If economic, social, environmental and political change were like the four legs of a table, social development—overcoming poverty and misery—would be the wobbliest leg.

The U.S. government consistently and actively promotes free markets and economic growth. It also, but less consistently, promotes democracy and environmental protection. But it is not at all consistent or persistent in its support for efforts to overcome hunger and poverty.

Those of us who want a world without hunger shouldn't take economic growth, democracy or environmental protection for granted. Continued progress in those areas is critically important to hungry people. But advocates need to push, in particular, for greater efforts to overcome hunger and poverty.

How massive would these extra efforts need to be?

A number of studies have attempted to determine the cost of huge improvements in human well-being and what share the United States might appropriately contribute. These cost estimates vary but none is prohibitive.

The World Summit for Children in 1990 set these global goals for the year 2000:

- 33 percent reduction in child deaths;
- 50 percent reduction in child malnutrition;
- 50 percent reduction in deaths of women during pregnancy and childbirth;
- universally available family planning;
- safe water and sanitation for all;
- basic education for all children;
- 90 percent immunization of children;

- eradication of polio;
- 95 percent reduction in measles deaths;
- 50 percent reduction in child deaths caused by diarrhea; and
- 33 percent reduction in child deaths from pneumonia.

UNICEF estimated that the cost of meeting these goals is $25 billion a year, which is about 12 days' worth of world military spending. Since poor people in developing countries have so little, the cost of big improvements in their lives is modest.

UNICEF suggested that the developing countries bear about half this $25 billion cost, and that the world's rich countries might divide the other half. A fair U.S. share might be about $2 billion a year.[1]

This was not an academic exercise. Many nations committed resources. With constant encouragement from Bread for the World, Results and others, the U.S. government increased its funding for child survival and related assistance programs. The world has, in fact, made notable progress toward the World Summit for Children goals during the 1990s. For example, 80 percent of all children in developing countries were immunized against the six major child-killing diseases in 1998, up from only 5 percent in 1980. Polio will be eliminated by the year 2000, thus saving the governments of the world about $1.5 billion a year in vaccine treatment and rehabilitation costs.[2]

In 1998, the U.N. Development Program estimated the cost of extending basic nutrition, health care, education, water and sanitation to all the world's people at $40 billion a year.[3] That is less than 4 percent of the combined wealth of the 225 richest people in the world.

Also in 1998, the U.S. Agency for International Development (USAID) commissioned a study of what it would cost to meet the World Food Summit goal of cutting world hunger in half by the year 2015 and what the U.S. government's role should be in attaining that reduction. If current levels of response continue, the study projected that the number of hungry people might increase to about 910 million in 2015. Analysts estimated that it would cost $45 billion over 15 years to reduce the number of hungry people to 400 million by 2015. This was based on the actual results of different types of USAID projects in specific countries. $45 billion over 15 years comes to $3 billion a year, of which a fair share for the United States, they said, might be about $685 million.[4]

These estimates are clearly very rough:

UNICEF	Dramatic gains for children	$25 billion a year
UNDP	Nutrition, health and education for all	$40 billion a year
USAID	Reducing hunger by half	$ 3 billion a year

But they suggest that the U.S. government could well afford to do its part to overcome hunger. If the cost of ending widespread hunger were as much as $50 billion a year, a fair share for the U.S. government might be five billion dollars. That's less than one-half of 1 percent of the federal budget. People in the United States spend $8 billion each year on cosmetics.[5]

While UNICEF, UNDP and USAID focused on additional spending, more than that is required. Changes that give poor and hungry people opportunities to shape decisions are also necessary. Community organizers around the world are working from the bottom up to empower poor people, and top-down shifts such as the World Bank's growing emphasis on consultation with low-income communities also help. Changes in economic systems, such as the inclusion of labor rights in trade agreements, are crucial too. Finally, political change needs to be complemented by myriad private initiatives, such as mass-media attention, business enterprise, voluntary assistance and redoubled efforts by hungry and poor people themselves to seize emerging opportunities.

Government spending alone won't overcome hunger, but these cost estimates are suggestive of the level of effort required. They show that overcoming widespread hunger in the world is affordable. In comparison to what affluent people and nations spend on many other things, overcoming world hunger is scandalously cheap.

How much would it cost to overcome hunger in the United States?

In 1990, Bread for the World and many other organizations jointly issued the Medford Declaration. After considerable study and debate, the organizations agreed that the United States could end widespread hunger and food insecurity within its own borders simply by increasing allocations to the national nutrition programs—mainly food stamps, WIC and school meals. These programs are proven, relatively efficient and underfunded.

The estimated cost of expanding these programs enough to ensure food security for all U.S. households was about ten billion dollars a year.[6] That figure is more, on a per capita basis, than the UNICEF or USAID estimates for meeting basic nutrition needs in poor countries, because the cost of living in the United States is much higher than in developing countries, and so is the standard for hunger.

In 1996, Congress and the president instead slashed food programs by roughly five billion dollars a year. So as of today, annual spending on the national nutrition programs might have to increase by *roughly* $15 billion per year to end U.S. hunger.

The Medford Declaration also urged measures to encourage better job prospects for low-income people. That is a better and more durable way to end hunger than nutrition programs. An additional $15 billion annually would expand job training and placement, child care to make it easier for parents to go to work, health insurance for all low-income children (so that parents who must take jobs without benefits don't have to choose between working and health insurance for their children) and improvements in education (so the next generation of workers is better prepared to earn a decent wage).

The authors aren't wedded to a particular approach to ending hunger in the United States, and they don't believe that government spending is all that's needed. Policies that strengthen the economy and give poor people more influence over programs and policies that affect them are also important. They don't think for a minute that the federal government can do it all. The private sector, state and local governments and society as a whole, including poor people, must do their parts to end hunger.

But these rough calculations suggest the level of effort required and show that overcoming hunger in the United States is affordable. Fifteen billion dollars for nutrition programs plus $15 billion to help people get decent jobs comes to a total of $30 billion a year. If the U.S. share in overcoming hunger worldwide is about five billion dollars, the total annual cost of overcoming hunger worldwide and in our own country would be about $35 billion.

If the cost would turn out to be $50 billion a year, that would amount to less than one percent of our national income. It's about 3 percent of the federal budget. In 1998, the U.S. government ran a budget surplus of $70 billion. People in the United States spend $50 billion a year going to the movies.

No one knows exactly what initiatives will get us to the goal, and no one knows exactly what it will cost. Bread for the World Institute's annual hunger report for the year 2000[7] suggests a more fully developed program to end hunger. But it's already clear that the necessary level of effort is affordable, even modest. Ending widespread hunger in the United States and worldwide is well within our reach. We are a *rich* nation and we do not need to act like paupers when it comes to something so basic, so fundamentally just, as ending hunger.

Chapter 26

Transforming the Politics of Hunger

> High politics is not the art of the possible; it is the art of enlarging what is possible and making what has hereto been impossible come in the range of what can be considered.
>
> —*William Lee Miller*[1]

Culture and politics in the United States could be changed enough to win the commitment needed to overcome hunger at home and abroad. There are already strong indications of public concern. A series of polls commissioned by the Second Harvest network of food banks show that the U.S. public ranks hunger as one of the nation's seven most important problems. More than half of all Americans say they want the government to spend more on programs to assist hungry people, and another third want the government to maintain its current efforts. Only one in eight Americans want the government to spend less on programs to assist hungry people.[2]

Surveys about foreign aid have repeatedly found that the U.S. public, by large margins, supports assistance to people who are hungry and poor as well as environmental aid to poor countries. Foreign aid spending is unpopular, partly because people doubt whether U.S. foreign aid effectively serves humanitarian purposes.[3]

Events in some other countries have been encouraging, too. All of the other industrial nations do more to reduce poverty among their own children and in poor countries than the United States does. People in countries like France, Germany, Holland and Sweden have worked for decades to build political support for social programs and international development assistance. Some nations with much lower levels of average income—countries as diverse as Costa Rica, Botswana, and China—demonstrate more political will to reduce hunger and poverty than the United States does. Each country has to tackle the goal of ending hunger in its own way. But if people in other countries have the political will to reduce hunger and poverty, why not in this country?

This chapter outlines ten lines of action that together could mobilize the political commitment needed to eliminate widespread hunger. Millions of people and tens of thousands of organizations in the United States are already making some effort to reduce hunger and poverty, domestically or worldwide. If part of this effort were redirected from relatively low-impact activities to these ten priorities, widespread hunger could be ended.

1. Religious communities can teach how social concern flows from a relationship with God and can help motivate involvement in effective political action.

Some religious people show relatively little concern about people in need, and most churches fail to teach their people to let God's passion for justice shape their politics. On the other hand, virtually every religious tradition insists on sharing with the poor and the hungry, and members of congregations also tend to be more charitable.[4]

The Roman Catholic Church and most Protestant denominations maintain major programs of assistance, education and advocacy. The Presbyterian Church (USA), Evangelical Lutheran Church in America, Lutheran Church–Missouri Synod, United Methodist Church, Reformed Church in America, Christian Reformed Church, United Church of Christ, American Baptist Church, Southern Baptist Church, Cooperative Baptist Fellowship, Reorganized Church of Latter-Day Saints, Evangelical Covenant Church and other denominations maintain major programs of education and funding focused specifically on hunger. Churches, synagogues and mosques probably do more than any other institutions in U.S. society to teach social concern and take on otherwise neglected problems of poverty. Nearly all churches help their members to know and care about needs in the poorer parts of the world.

Bread for the World itself is evidence that people motivated

Pontius' Puddle

by the Christian gospel can change politics. The organization's distinctive strength is its uniquely large and active network of grassroots advocates. These local leaders demonstrate remarkable persistence, often with only limited support from Bread for the World's small staff. The secret of Bread for the World's grassroots strength is Christian faith. Nearly all of its grassroots leaders feel called by God and are, to some extent, encouraged by their churches.

The experience of God's grace in Jesus Christ is already bringing many hungry people to the table, as Christian people are moved to serve and become advocates. We pray that God's grace will work yet more powerfully in the hearts and churches of this nation—to tip the balance of U.S. politics and end mass hunger in God's world.

Even when Christian churches seem inert, they carry the biblical witness about a gracious God. The authors, both Christian pastors, have seen the power that the word of God has in the lives of people. It can even turn the heart of a materialistic, self-centered nation toward people in need.

2. Individuals and agencies assisting hungry people can expand what they do to influence government policies.

Millions of people are already participating in private food banks, food pantries and other assistance agencies, mostly by contributing a bit of money or food. These people care about hunger and poverty. Some are already involved in advocacy, but most are not. If just 5 or 10 percent of these concerned people would speak up for hungry people in a united way, elected officials would respond. If, in addition, these agencies could equip just 5 or 10 percent of the people they help to speak up for themselves politically, a mass movement would be launched. Similarly, if just 5 or 10 percent of the millions of people who contribute to assistance abroad would also convey their concerns to members of Congress, U.S. policies toward developing countries would change in a big way.

Charities can address public policy issues with credibility and insight. Many have begun to speak out. Since 1990, tax regulations have clearly allowed charities to devote a significant share of their budgets to lobbying. Sweeping setbacks for poor people—the debt crisis and foreign aid cuts internationally, growing hunger and assistance cuts domestically—have also pushed charities toward involvement in public policy.

InterAction, the association of private agencies that provide international assistance, has over the last ten years become an important voice in Congress on foreign aid issues. All the major U.S. charities—Second Harvest, Catholic Charities, Lutheran Services of America, the Salvation Army and others—now speak up on public policy issues and make at least some effort to educate their supporters. But this is just a beginning.

3. Antihunger advocacy organizations can be extended and strengthened.

The authors hope that every reader of this book will join Bread for the World, but you can also work effectively through other advocacy organizations. Network is a Catholic social justice organization with an agenda that includes hunger along with other issues. Results is an effective, secular grassroots lobby for hungry people. The Roman Catholic Church, the National Council of Churches and some Protestant denominations maintain grassroots advocacy networks.

You can also join groups that speak up for children, the environment, peace or other related issues. Groups that speak up for poor people in state capitals are especially needed now that some important social policy decisions are being made by the states. The Catholic and Lutheran churches have networks of state advocacy offices, and state and local councils of churches are also active in state-level advocacy.

4. Low-income people's organizations can be strengthened, especially in their capacity to influence government policies that affect poor people.

Bread for the World and other advocacy organizations are often overwhelmed by larger, self-interested political forces. Hunger in the United States will not disappear until low-income people become a more active political force. Millions of low-income voters would make a difference, especially since people are usually most forceful in defending their own interests. But low-income people tend to be swamped by the day-to-day challenges of survival, and they are usually less educated than others; so dealing with national policy issues can be difficult for them. They often assume that their opinions won't make any difference to public officials.

However, community organizing among low-income people seems to be on the upswing. Local churches and other community organizations identify a need, build an organization to address it, and then push for change at the local or state level. The Industrial Areas Foundation, the Center for Community Change, and the Campaign for Human Development are among the key national organizations that support community organizing.

Voter registration drives in low-income communities have an influence on both local and national elections. Churches in low-income communities can also invite candidates to listen to community concerns or take part in Bread for the World campaigns.

The worldwide shift toward democracy in the 1980s and 1990s has allowed organizations to grow in low-income communities worldwide. They take many forms—neighborhood groups, religious groups, labor unions, sometimes local governments. A primary thrust of Bread for the World's international work has been to urge the World Bank and USAID to involve poor people and local advocates in developing countries in the design of projects and policies.

5. Organizations of people of color can be strengthened, and other organizations that help low-income people can more fully engage people of color.

The proportion of those who go hungry is higher among African Americans, Latinos and Native Americans. Even many prosperous persons of color know discrimination firsthand, and this can give them a sense of solidarity with low-income people. Racism and hunger are intertwined, so progress on one front helps on the other. Thus, strengthening organizations like the NAACP and the National Council of La Raza is part of antihunger politics. Historically black colleges, African American and Latino churches and local ethnic organizations also play key roles.

People of color bring valuable experience and intensity into charities and other antihunger organizations. Bread for the World has long been committed to racial diversity in its board, staff and membership. Cultivating racial diversity takes sustained effort, but it is worth it.

6. The media can move beyond stories of pity and charity to explain the causes of hunger, and people and organizations concerned about hunger can make a bigger effort to influence the media.

The media are more influential than ever, but they devote little attention to hunger, and their hunger coverage is typically limited to stories of pity and charity. The power of the media, especially television, has increased the cost of political campaigns and made money a more important factor in elections.

But the media can also be a potent ally in the struggle against hunger. When Bread for the World Institute surveyed 50 of the largest and most influential organizations in the country that work against hunger and poverty, it found that they devote little staff time to media work. What's more, nine-tenths of their media work is focused on promoting themselves rather than on explaining hunger and what can be done about it.[5] That's one reason why media coverage tends to focus on pity and charity: "Look at this poor family and the wonderful way our local charity is helping them," or "Look at this helpless African country and the heroic efforts of U.S. relief workers."

Bread for the World has found that any concerned individual, with a little training, can influence how local newspapers and radio stations cover hunger issues. Just a few staff members in Bread for the World's national office can sometimes win significant coverage of hunger issues in national media.

7. Students, colleges and universities can be enlisted in the struggle against hunger and poverty.

Today's college students are often engaged in community service, and that experience can open perceptive young eyes to the need for structural reforms. At present, most students remain skeptical about government and are scarcely aware of the possibilities of advocacy. Yet successful movements for social change almost always include university students and faculty. Anti-hunger politics needs the intellectual power of universities and the energy and lifelong commitment of students.

Oxfam and the National Student Campaign Against Hunger and Homelessness have campus networks that help students get involved in efforts to reduce international and domestic hunger. Bread for the World also has a campus organizer and contacts on hundreds of campuses, helping students and faculty influence Congress on hunger issues. Typically, a campus religious or service group adds Bread for the World advocacy to its other activities.

8. A clear and fresh antihunger policy agenda should be developed that can draw people from across political and ideological lines.

The child-survival revolution and microenterprise development are relatively new ideas that have won widespread political support and are making big contributions toward the end of hunger. To end hunger, we need more fresh thinking.

The world has changed. The globalization of the economy puts pressure on all governments to reduce taxes and social spending. It also puts low-skilled workers in competition with each other. This makes efforts to expand government social programs more difficult than before, and renders strategies to enhance the earning capacity of low-income workers more important than before.

At the same time, people in the United States and around the world are insisting on more control of their lives and a stronger role for local institutions. This is partly because the population of most countries, including our own, is better educated. This change in sensibilities opens up possibilities to shift from top-down, bureaucratic social programs to bottom-up, community-based initiatives.

The 1996 welfare reform bill gained wide public acceptance, not because it cut food stamps (a feature that got relatively little attention), but mainly because it promised to move people from welfare to jobs and shift responsibilities to state governments. A handful of conservative think tanks contributed greatly to the development and marketing of these ideas. Antihunger advocates must focus on jobs and decentralization just as creatively.

9. Voters and political leaders can inject hunger and poverty concerns into electoral politics, so that elected officials more often provide leadership in overcoming hunger.

The importance of electoral politics became clearer than ever in the 1990s. In earlier decades, there was bipartisan support for many antihunger measures, such as food stamps or development aid for Africa. But in recent years, the Republican leadership in Congress has pushed hard to cut government spending, including these programs. The Democratic Party during the Clinton administration has moved away from speaking out for poor people.

Bread for the World does not endorse candidates for office, but it encourages its members to get involved in electoral politics—to vote, to ask questions of candidates in private and public meetings and to contribute time and money to campaigns and political parties. Who gets elected and what each party stands for are tremendously important.

In 1996, Bread for the World focused its annual Offering of

Letters on candidates for Congress. Bread for the World members and churches asked candidates from all parties to commit themselves to helping to overcome widespread hunger among U.S. children. In all, 669 candidates signed the commitment, including 42 percent of the candidates who were eventually elected to Congress. Though it is hard to gauge the impact, this campaign may have helped somewhat to change the tone of Congress. The Congress elected in 1996 was not as hard on poor and hungry people as was the prior Congress.

This nation needs to elect leaders committed to moving people out of poverty. Imagine the two political parties accepting the challenge to end hunger at home and abroad and perhaps offering competing approaches to reach this goal. It could happen, if voters decide they want it to.

10. People and organizations working against poverty and hunger should think of themselves as parts of a large, potentially dynamic movement.

Thousands of U.S. organizations are dedicated to reducing hunger or to some related cause, but each tends to focus on its own work. When these groups think and act as a movement, they can coordinate and build on one another's efforts. Such strategic thinking almost always nudges assistance agencies to get more involved in the politics of hunger.

Bread for the World works to build the larger movement against hunger. At the national level, Bread for the World has helped to increase collaboration among domestic antihunger organizations and among international assistance agencies. In both cases, increased cooperation has encouraged assistance agencies to get more involved in lobbying Congress. In a number of states and communities, Bread for the World Institute has convened leaders from diverse antihunger and antipoverty networks. In every instance, a stronger sense of movement and long-term purpose has led organizations to become more effective in public education and advocacy.

Individuals and agencies do a lot to help people in need. But galvanized as a movement, these individuals and agencies could transform the politics of hunger. The level of effort required to overcome hunger is affordable, and the political change required to launch and sustain an effort to overcome hunger is also feasible.

Of course, people of good will may try and, in the end, fail to win the necessary political change. Even though dramatic reductions in hunger are quite feasible, politicians and public opinion may never be moved enough to seize this God-given opportunity. But even if we fail to overcome hunger, we will surely make life better for many than if we did nothing.

In any case, failure is not something we need to worry about. God has called us to be faithful. If we are faithful, if we lend our lives to a cause that is close to the heart of God, we can leave the matter of success to God.

Taking Action

Chapter 27

The Recovery of Vision

> Where there is no vision, the people perish.
> —*Proverbs 29:18 KJV*

The United States of America urgently needs a renewed commitment to justice for poor and hungry people.

Everyone needs vision, and so does every nation. That means having a sense of direction, a sense of what the nation wants to do, what its special contribution should be. The United States had that at its founding. It was a bold and exciting new venture in a government of the people; and making that venture successful was a visionary undertaking, one that made this nation "a city set on a hill" for much of the world. The struggle epitomized by the Civil War and later the civil rights movement focused on an unfulfilled aspect of the founding vision: that all people are created equal. The Great Depression, World War II and the Cold War in turn compelled the nation to overcome epic threats to its way of life. In each phase of the nation's history, citizens rallied around visions, which shaped its history.

Today there is much that is great and good about the United States, but also much that is troubling. In some respects the founding experiment has been an astonishing success. Since the end of the Cold War it has enjoyed an extended period of relative peace and prosperity, and the United States has become the most affluent and powerful nation on earth.

Yet the nation has also become more fragmented, more driven by special interests, more attuned to a culture of violence, more stressed by family breakdown, less civil in its discourse and more cynical about its government. Hunger has been on the increase. Could it be that individualism has become the nation's Achilles' heel, that individual liberty, detached from a sense of responsibility for justice and the common good, is ultimately destructive?

If so, what does that mean?

It elevates the importance of the common good. The United States is "one nation, under God, indivisible, with liberty and justice for all." That underscores a sense of community. It combines liberty with justice. The lessons of the nation's past say that liberty and justice cannot be secured for some people and kept from others without turning sour. Because it has cherished liberty, the United States has sacrificed in lives and material resources enormously, if not always wisely. But it has not cherished justice as much. Yet justice no less than liberty is one of the nation's founding ideals. The pursuit of justice for poor and hungry people, both nationally and internationally, should become a higher aspiration.

Where does that higher aspiration lead us?

First, into prayer and reflection. People need to ask God to stir up a longing for justice in their own hearts, within their churches and within the nation.

Second, the Holy Spirit, who instills in hearts a longing for justice, is already at work within us. Tens of millions of people give time or money to help others in need. Millions belong to organizations that work on issues important to poverty, the environment or related concerns. So the nation is not starting from scratch.

If a desire for justice and the common good grows, charitable and civic activities will also grow, and more people involved in those activities will appeal to their elected officials for action. Low-income communities and disadvantaged racial groups will become more engaged in civic life. Leaders of both political parties would respond. The country would be within striking distance of galvanizing the will needed to overcome hunger.

With so many causes that need support, why should people focus on hunger?

When people focus on hunger they focus on those who are *most* in need, because food is essential to life. Who can deny that it is not right to let people go hungry? That is why the problem of hunger engages a wide array of people from different political and religious points of view.

Hunger is connected to other social challenges—peace, the environment, revitalizing democracy, economic justice and more. It serves as a lens for seeing the health or lack of health of society as a whole. Work to overcome hunger draws us together with people whose main focus is peace, the environment, poverty or children.

The feasibility of ending widespread hunger also makes it a compelling issue. Hunger could be virtually eliminated in the United States within a few years, and most hunger worldwide within a few decades. That would be a giant stride toward the ideal of "justice for all."

The feasibility of ending hunger and the injustice of letting it continue make this cause analogous to the nineteenth-century movement to end slavery.

William Wilberforce was a young member of the British Parliament. With the help of a core of fellow evangelical Christians, Wilberforce succeeded in getting Parliament to abolish the slave trade in 1806. It took 27 additional years of struggling against the odds until, just four days before his death on 29 July 1833, the efforts of Wilberforce and his cohorts, together with the rising support of public opinion, finally paid off. Parliament brought the scandal of slavery to an end throughout the British Empire.

John Newton was a slave trader who repented, founded a society for the abolition of slavery and became pastor of a church in London that served as a meeting place for Wilberforce and his colleagues. Newton wrote:

> Amazing grace! How sweet the sound,
> that saved a wretch like me;
> I once was lost, but now am found,
> was blind but now I see.

Amazing grace not only saved Wilberforce and Newton, but turned their lives against the evil of slavery, and eventually an empire was moved to abolish it. In the same way God's grace, no less amazing today, can move people to shake this nation and the world to overcome the scandal of hunger.

What would a commitment to justice mean to me personally?

If we can overcome hunger, everyone—including our children and grandchildren—will live in a better, safer and more prosperous world.

But commitment to justice also offers spiritual rewards, because we cannot truly know God if we turn aside from those who are poor and hungry. "I hate, I despise your [religious] festivals," said the Lord through the prophet Amos to an affluent people who loved to pray, while doing little about poor people who were being trampled. "But let justice roll down like waters, and righteousness like an ever-flowing stream" (Am 5:21, 24).

Just as the nation needs vision, we as individuals need vision. We need to live for a purpose bigger than ourselves. Self-centered lives are not happy lives.

Jesus said, "Those who want to save their life will lose it; and those who lose their life for my sake and for the sake of the gospel, will save it" (Mk 8:35). Jesus calls us to lay down our lives for others, because he laid down his life for us. This is the life that trumps death.

Saying *Yes!* to God's call for justice becomes a celebration of God's grace toward us and others. We are not saved by the work of justice, but we are created in Christ Jesus for that purpose, along with other works of love, and therefore it is the way of joy.

Chapter 28

You Can Make a Difference!

> The only thing necessary for the triumph of evil is for good men to do nothing.
> —*Edmund Burke*[1]

The single most important factor needed to end hunger is the commitment, the will, to do it. That's true for the individual, and it's true for the nation and the world. Once a firm, enduring commitment has been made, there are many ways to build upon it. The will comes first. The rest follows.

For those who want to see hunger eliminated, the biggest obstacle to making a commitment toward that end is the feeling, especially when it comes to crucial policy matters, that "what I do won't make any difference." This pervasive, disempowering myth holds us back. It is wrong. It is wrong because it defies evidence to the contrary. And it is wrong theologically.

It is wrong theologically because to say, "What I do won't make any difference," is to accept the counsel of despair, and despair is unbelief. The God of the Bible moves in history to free slaves, give them land to till, overthrow oppression and call people into mission. Bread for the World members look at current history from the perspective of hungry people and often see—or think they see—God's saving power at work. Doors open, hearts open, good things happen, and they thank God.

Giving in to the feeling of powerlessness is also ingratitude for the gift of influence that all U.S. citizens have. In fact, U.S. citizens in this post–Cold War period have more power and freedom to influence the global order for the good of others than any other group of people in modern times. That gives us an *extraordinary* opportunity, surely one that God would have us use to bring justice to those living in hunger and poverty.

The text of choice is the parable of the talents in Matthew 25, in which Jesus condemns the arrogance and cowardice of the servant who buried his master's treasure—feigning powerlessness rather than putting it in service to the master. The nature of the service that we are to do for our Master is not left in doubt, for the parable is immediately followed by Jesus' description of the final judgment, in which he welcomes those who have fed the hungry and condemns those who have not.

What evidence contradicts the view that "What I do won't make any difference"?

The experience the authors know best is that of Bread for the World. Every year since 1975, a relatively modest number of letters from each congressional district across the land has convinced our nation's leaders to act in ways that make a huge difference for a large number of hungry people.

Consider Africa, where hungry people have few defenders in Congress. Bread for the World's 1995 campaign to protect crucial development aid to Africa mobilized approximately 70 thousand letters and reduced by about $100 million the cuts that took place. In this case the average letter leveraged more than one thousand dollars to Africans in dire need.

In 1991, Bread for the World mobilized 100 thousand letters and helped get the U.S. State Department to mediate a peace agreement in Ethiopia that saved half a million lives. By any reasonable calculation, each letter in that campaign saved at least one life.

One person can make a difference for the hungry people in this country, too. In 1998 Congress and the president acted to restore food stamps to about 250 thousand of the most vulnerable legal immigrants—children, elderly and disabled people. This will give them $818 million in food assistance over a five-year period. Bread for the World worked in coalition with many other groups to make this happen. But without the roughly 70 thousand letters that Bread for the World members sent, Congress would not have approved this measure.

The letters secured a broad base of congressional support. They included 700 letters from students at Villanova University, near Philadelphia, where Andrea Maresca learned about Bread for the World during a class with Dr. Suzanne Toton, professor of theology and religious studies, and decided to start a campus chapter. One result was 700 letters to Pennsylvania's U.S. senators, a major contribution, because a key step in the campaign was to get the president to include funding in his budget proposal to restore food stamps to legal immigrants. Bread for the World's strategy was to get a Republican senator to take a leadership role in lining up support from Senate colleagues for an appeal to the president. Arlen Specter of Pennsylvania was favorably disposed to the bill, but a far higher commitment was needed from him—his leadership. Letters came to him from Bread for the World members all over Pennsylvania. The student group at Villanova University was especially active, and a class of high school students came from Philadelphia to visit Senator Specter's office. Then Alan Shawn Feinstein and a handful of other individuals and churches placed ads in four Philadelphia newspapers.

Without the initiative of these advocates, Specter would not have organized a Senate letter to the president. And until President Clinton received that letter, his administration was not considering the restoration of food stamps to legal immigrants. Each letter to Congress on this issue had the effect, on average, of helping two or three immigrants receive their daily bread for five years—quite a return for writing a letter.

Does Bread for the World have defeats as well as victories?

Of course. Sometimes programs that Bread for the World has worked for years to build up and improve, like WIC, food stamps or development aid to Africa, get slashed or threatened. That's frustrating. Yet we are called to "defend the rights of the poor," (Prv 31:9) and without that defense hunger and poverty would be much worse. Some years members of Bread for the World watch Congress and the president make decisions that cause despair among poor and vulnerable people.

In fact, hunger has been increasing in the United States since Bread for the World began in 1974. There is nothing inevitable about future progress against hunger. Public opinion and elected officials may opt to let more and more people go hungry. But our experience so far is that, even when the political climate is most difficult, a few committed people can achieve a lot for hungry people through advocacy.

Why are people reluctant to write or contact decision makers about key policies?

One reason is that they've never done it and are intimidated, though in reality it is quite easy. Another is that public policy, compared to direct assistance, seems remote and abstract. Millard Fuller, founder and president of Habitat for Humanity, says that one of the reasons Habitat has grown so dramatically is that the idea is tangible. You can swing a hammer, pound some nails and afterward take a picture of a house. People, he says, will support anything they can take a picture of. But public policy is hard to take a picture of, even though it impacts millions of lives. A soup kitchen, a food pantry, a hungry child, a village school— all are friendlier to the camera. Besides, helping out in a soup kitchen, bringing food to a pantry or contributing to an agency that does direct assistance gives one an immediate sense of satisfaction, a way of measuring benefits to a child or a family. Advocating more humane policies rarely offers that quick, measurable satisfaction.

In addition, public policy is far more complex, and for that reason it is often controversial. People tend to avoid complexity and controversy.

For many Christians public policy has no business in the church—as they said about slavery and the rise of Hitler. It seems to violate the separation of church and state or at least intrude on the church's mission to preach the gospel. But this view confuses the separation of church and state with the separation of faith from life. If Christ is Lord, then all of life, including our responsibilities as citizens, fall under his lordship. And if large areas of life, such as economic decisions that have a great bearing on the welfare of those most vulnerable, are off limits to faith, then we have excluded Christ and the gospel from much of life. Clearly, if responding effectively to the call of God regarding hungry people means advocating policy changes, then we must allow that God is inviting us to do so.

There is also vast skepticism, even cynicism, about government, and plenty of apathy abroad in the land. These, too, can suck us in and make us part of the problem rather than part of the solution.

Isn't it money rather than citizen opinion that calls the shots in U.S. politics today?

Money has become important. Campaigns are expensive. On average, each U.S. senator has to raise about $2,300 every day (seven days a week, 365 days a year) during a six-year term to finance the next campaign.[2] One result is that special interests, like tobacco companies or health care providers, increase their influence by contributing to political campaigns. In addition, the annual cost of all Washington-based lobbying comes to about one billion dollars.[3]

A study of individuals who contributed $200 or more to congressional candidates in 1996 found that 95 percent were white, 80 percent were men, and 81 percent had annual family incomes above $100 thousand. Twenty percent had annual incomes higher than $500 thousand.[4] Campaign donors or potential donors get better access to politicians than most citizens. It's difficult for citizens from big states to meet personally with their senators. One Senate staffer reported getting a hundred phone calls a day, more than could possibly be returned. "So," the staff member said, "I'll *try* to get back to Bread for the World . . . [but] I *will* get back to a donor."[5]

The power of money underscores all the more the importance of citizen action, because elected officials still depend on voters. In the authors' judgment, most elected officials are decent human beings who intend to serve the public good. Voters back home typically get agitated about matters of self-interest. Elected officials are sometimes delighted when voters back home ask them to do something for hungry people.

If advocacy for hungry people works so well, how can more be engaged to do it?

That's our great challenge and, frankly, our purpose in writing this book. We want to enlist *you* and thousands of others in the cause against hunger. When we see what a difference 44 thousand Bread for the World advocates make, we are convinced that a doubling or tripling of advocates would multiply their impact exponentially and change the outcome on policy decisions. We would also be much closer to creating the critical mass necessary to turn the ending of hunger into a national and international commitment.

Okay, I'm persuaded. But my time is limited. I can't devote my life to it—maybe one or two hours a month. How do I get involved?

We thought you'd never ask. Please turn the page. The next chapter tells more about Bread for the World and ways you can get involved.

Chapter 29
Bread for the World

> Hunger results more from human choices than from natural disasters. . . . Your reports provide important lessons about the complex realities of our world.
>
> —*Former President Jimmy Carter*

> Bread for the World is a strong and respected voice on Capitol Hill for those who suffer from hunger at home and around the world.
>
> —*U.S. Senator Olympia Snowe (R-Maine)*

Bread for the World is a nationwide Christian citizens' movement whose members seek justice for hungry people by lobbying the nation's decision makers. Year after year, it wins legislative victories that deliver substantial benefits to hungry people. As a result, *Bread for the World members offer hope and opportunity to hungry people.*

How does Bread for the World work?

Its 44 thousand members contact their representatives in Congress about legislation that affects hungry people in the United States or worldwide. Thousands of local churches, student campaigns and community groups support Bread for the World with letters to Congress and financial gifts. Some members meet locally to pray, study and take action. Some meet with their representatives in Congress, organize telephone trees, win media coverage and reach out to new churches. But most members simply write an occasional well-timed letter to Congress.

Bread for the World is the nation's largest grassroots advocacy network on international development issues and one of the largest on domestic hunger and poverty issues.

Bread for the World is supported by more than 40 denominations, and its membership reflects great diversity. Catholics,

Bread for the World's Recent Offerings of Letters

1991 The Horn of Africa

Bread for the World's Horn of Africa Law has saved hundreds of thousands of lives. It encouraged the United States to broker a peace agreement in Ethiopia, provided aid and prohibits U.S. aid to dictators in the region.

1992 Every Fifth Child

Bread for the World helped win almost $2 billion in increases for WIC, Head Start and Job Corps in 1992 and 1993, benefiting about a million infants, mothers and children.

1993 Many Neighbors, One Earth

Sustainable development—the reduction of hunger and poverty in environmentally sound ways—became a prominent purpose of the U.S. administration's foreign aid policy. Funding for poverty-focused aid was cut less than military and security aid during 1993 and 1994.

1994 A Child Is Waiting

Bread for the World helped win a $260 million increase for WIC in 1994 and again in 1995.

mainline and evangelical Protestants, Orthodox and some who are not church members join together to speak out against hunger.

Bread for the World includes Republicans, Democrats and Independents. Neither major party consistently defends poor and hungry people, so Bread for the World brings together conservatives and liberals from both parties around practical actions that make gains against hunger.

1995 Africa: Crisis to Opportunity

Congress slashed development assistance, but Bread for the World helped protect at least $100 million in aid to Africa.

1996 Elect to End Childhood Hunger

Bread for the World helped maintain the national food stamps program, but Congress slashed funding for it and other anti-poverty programs. Nearly 700 candidates committed themselves to support federal legislation to help overcome childhood hunger that fall, including 42 percent of those who won election.

1997 Tell Congress: Hunger Has a Cure

Bread for the World helped restore $3 billion for nutrition programs in 1997 and 1998, providing assistance for about 650,000 people.

1998 Africa: Seeds of Hope

The Africa: Seeds of Hope Act became law. It redirected U.S. aid and investment toward agriculture and rural development in Africa. It also helped assure that the United States maintains a stock of grain for humanitarian emergencies.

Bread for the World has a partner organization, Bread for the World Institute, which carries out research and education on hunger. The Institute's annual report on world hunger, for example, strengthens the antihunger movement with careful analysis of causes and solutions to hunger. This book is also an Institute project.

Bread for the World's board of directors includes grassroots leaders, members of Congress and leaders of churches and charities. The majority of directors are elected by Bread for the World's members.

Bread for the World collaborates with hundreds of other organizations to build a movement that can win the changes needed to end widespread hunger.

What makes Bread for the World work is people like you. There are four basic ways to take part: become a member, contribute financially, involve your church and become an activist.

1. Become a member.

Joining Bread for the World helps you make the most of the limited time you have for acting as a citizen against hunger. When you write or call your members of Congress, other Bread for the World members across the country are doing the same. Good timing and clarity of message multiply the impact.

Bread for the World's newsletter, action alerts and web site (http://www.bread.org) give you concise, reliable information on legislation in Congress that is important to hungry people. You know when your representatives serve on key committees and how they vote on hunger issues. You get educational resources (fact sheets, devotional aids and background papers) that will strengthen your effectiveness as an advocate for hungry people.

2. Contribute financially.

The basic membership contribution is $25 a year ($15 for students). If you can't afford that, give what you can. The authors, of course, hope you will give more. Three-quarters of Bread for the World's budget comes from its members.

Typically, each dollar in our own budget secures more than $100 for hungry people. Bread for the World gets this extraordinarily high return by "leveraging" each dollar twice. A small staff supports a volunteer network of active citizens and they, in turn, influence how the government uses its massive resources and power.

Because Bread for the World lobbies Congress on behalf of hungry people, contributions to Bread for the World are not tax deductible. Contributions to Bread for the World Institute go to research and education, so they *are* tax deductible.

Rick Steves, host of a public television series on budget travel, is an enthusiastic Bread for the World donor:

> Bread for the World is my personal miracle of loaves and fishes. Through Bread, God uses the active citizenship of Christian people to multiply the benefits of our gifts to help hungry people. Speaking as an expert in getting the most out of every dollar, I give Bread for the World three stars.

3. Involve your church.

You can enhance the life of your church and make a big difference for hungry people by getting your church involved in Bread for the World. You might ask your church to participate in Bread for the World's annual Offering of Letters. Some churches allow time for letter writing in a worship service, or at least have people place their letters in an offering basket that is brought forward during worship. This action teaches everyone in church that letters to Congress are a fit offering to God and that citizenship is part of stewardship. Other churches set up a letter-writing table during the coffee hour or present the Offering of Letters in Sunday school or to a social concerns committee. An annual Offering of Letters kit provides everything needed to make any church's offering of letters a success.

About 1,000 churches have become Bread for the World Covenant Churches. They agree to make hunger a significant focus of ministry, participate in letter writing and support Bread for the World financially. Or, short of that commitment, another way to involve your church is to ask the mission or social concerns committee to make a financial contribution to Bread for the World.

Bread for the World offers resources to strengthen the hunger ministry of your church. These include a book of prayers and hymns on hunger and justice, a powerful musical about Lazarus that any church can produce, a special newsletter that helps churches do hunger advocacy as often as once a month, and much more. But the key to getting a church involved is typically that one or two members of the church feel called by God to help their fellow church members connect faith, citizenship and hunger.

4. Become an activist.

Because people like you step forward to become volunteer leaders, Bread for the World is a lively grass-roots presence in hundreds of communities. You might want to join or form a Bread for the World group in your church, college or community. Bread for the World members who meet together learn and draw strength from each other. They become more active. Many grow in faith and discipleship by meeting and praying with others who understand the connections between Jesus and justice. Some Bread for the World groups meet monthly. Others meet just a few times a year to take specific actions—to see their member of Congress, for example, or to plan a workshop for local churches on Bread's main campaign for the year.

Another possibility is to initiate or take part in a "quickline"—a telephone tree of people who call their members of Congress several times each year on urgent issues.

Are you willing to get information about hunger issues into your local newspaper or on television and radio? Bread for the World's media staff will help you shape public opinion and influence your members of Congress in this powerful way.

If you want to talk further about becoming a leader in the struggle to end hunger, call Bread for the World at 1-800-82-BREAD and ask for the organizer for your state.

And now you want to know, what will I do to help end hunger?

The authors hope you will join Bread for the World and have also suggested other ways you can help.

The important thing is to begin. Take a step, a small step. Then take another.

People of faith must act. Hundreds of millions are still excluded from the earth's banquet, but God wants to bring them to the table! And God has given us the awesome privilege of enabling more of them to come.

To do so is truly to celebrate grace at the table.

Resources

To contact your member of Congress, write or call:

Representative _____
U.S. House of Representatives
Washington, D.C. 20515   Phone: 202-224-3121

Senator _____
U.S. Senate
Washington, D.C. 20510   Phone: 202-224-3121

Bread for the World and Bread for the World Institute publish an array of resources for antihunger work, including:

- *Study Guide to* Grace at the Table (free). Will help you lead a study group on this book at your church.
- *Bread for the World* video ($8). A six-minute introduction to the organization.
- *Proclaim Jubilee: Break the Chains of Debt* ($7). A video and attractive, printed resources to help you and your church take part in a campaign to cancel unpayable debt for some of the world's poorest countries.
- *The Changing Politics of Hunger: Hunger 1999* ($18). Analysis of how the structures of politics are changing and how antihunger advocacy should adapt.
- *Banquet of Praise* by Joel Underwood ($2). A book of prayers and hymns on hunger and justice themes.
- *Lazarus* by Joel Underwood ($19.95). A musical designed for church productions.
- *For They Shall Be Fed* by Ron Sider ($10). Bible passages about hunger and justice.
- *Hunger Has a Cure* ($10). A CD-ROM for high school youth, prepared by the Presbyterian Church (USA).

Shipping and handling charges are $3.00 for orders under $25.00; $5.00 for orders from $25.00 to $49.99; and $7.00 for orders over $50.00. To order, or for information about other publications, call 1-800-82-BREAD, send an E-mail to publications@ bread.org. or visit Bread for the World's web site (http://www. bread.org). Through Bread for the World's web site, you can also connect to the web sites of various other organizations that provide information on hunger and justice issues.

Most church denominations maintain extensive programs of assistance, education and advocacy. Check with your church.

Notes

Chapter 1: A Place at the Table

1. The data in this chapter are more fully presented and documented in chapters 3 and 4.
2. Henry A. Kissinger, Address at the U.N. World Food Conference in Rome, 5–16 November 1974.
3. Presidential Commission on World Hunger, *Overcoming World Hunger: The Challenge Ahead* (Washington: U.S. Government Printing Office, 1980), x.

Chapter 2: What God Intends

1. In some cases we have used Today's English Version (TEV), the New Century Version (NCV) or the King James Version (KJV). Unless otherwise noted, biblical texts used in this book are from the New Revised Standard Version.
2. Paraphrased.
3. Independent Sector study, cited in "The Unrelenting Burdens of a Full-Time Church." *The New York Times*, 3 February 1995.

Chapter 3: World Hunger

1. From "The Arithmetic of Hunger," a poem from India, quoted in Presidential Commission on World Hunger, *Overcoming World Hunger: The Challenge Ahead* (Washington: U.S. Government Printing Office, 1980), 18.
2. Food Agriculture Organization (FAO) of the United Nations, "Information Note on Estimation of the Number of Undernourished," Paper Presented at the Committee on World Food Security, Twenty-fourth Session, Rome, 2–5 June 1998.
3. The World Bank, *Poverty Reduction and the World Bank* (Washington: The World Bank, 1996), 2, 4.
4. Tessa Wardlaw, Division of Evaluation, Policy and Planning, United Nations Children's Fund (UNICEF), personal communication to James Riker of Bread for the World Institute, 28 September 1998.
5. FAO, op. cit., 3, 7.
6. J. Dirck Stryker and Jeffrey C. Metzel, "Meeting the Food Summit Target: The United States Contribution" (Bethesda, Md.: Agricultural Policy Analysis Project, Phase III, September 1998), 3.
7. The GAO review and the U.S. Action Plan on Food Security are scheduled to be released in 1999.
8. FAO, op. cit.
9. "Mapping Undernutrition," an undated data chart from FAO.
10. James D. Wolfensohn, "The Other Crisis," address to the Board of Governors (Washington: The World Bank, 6 October 1998), 2.
11. James Gustave Speth, "Non-Benign Neglect," (New York: U.N. Development Program, 1998), 3.
12. Ibid., 2.
13. Wolfensohn, op. cit., 3.

14. Marc J. Cohen and Jashinta D'Costa, "Overview of World Hunger," *What Governments Can Do: Hunger 1997* (Silver Spring, Md.: Bread for the World Institute, 1996), 23.

15. Scott A. Leckman, "Grameen Bank Borrowers," *Pearls of Bangladesh*, ed. Marilyn Kodish (Washington: Results Educational Fund, 1993), 30–31.

16. Theresa Agovino, "Orphan Lives," *Worldview* 9, no. 4 (Fall 1996): 81.

17. Eugene Richards, "The Forgotten Ones," *Choices, The Human Development Magazine*, April 1998, 10–13.

Chapter 4: Hunger Next Door

1. U.S. Department of Agriculture (USDA), *Household Food Security in the United States in 1995*, (September 1997).

2. Carol S. Kramer-LeBlanc and Kathryn McMurry, eds., "Discussion Paper on Domestic Food Security," *Family Economics and Nutrition Reviews* (Washington: Center for Nutrition Policy and Promotion, USDA, II, nos. 1 and 2, 1998), 49.

3. U.S. Bureau of the Census, *Poverty in the United States: 1997* (September 1997).

4. The U.S. Department of Agriculture's Thrifty Food Plan provides the basis for determining the poverty line. On the tested assumption that poor people cannot ordinarily afford to spend more than one-third of their income on food, the government multiplies the cost of the Thrifty Food Plan diet by three. Studies have shown that even the least poor of the poor can barely afford this economy diet, and many low-income people above the poverty line cannot do so. Poverty in the United States, by definition, describes those usually unable to feed themselves adequately without some additional help.

5. U.S. Bureau of the Census, op. cit.

6. Mary Naifeh, "Trap Door? Revolving Door? Or Both?" *Current Population Reports: Household Economic Studies* (1998), 3.

7. U.S. Bureau of the Census, op. cit.

8. Richard A. Hoehn, "Feeding People: Half of Overcoming Hunger," *Transforming the Politics of Hunger: Hunger 1994*, ed. Marc J. Cohen (Silver Spring, Md.: Bread for the World Institute, 1993), 12.

9. Lynette Engelhardt, "Hunger in a Booming Economy," Bread for the World Background Paper #142 (September 1998).

10. Catholic Charities USA, *State Welfare Reform Project: Summary of Parish Social Ministries Welfare Reform Survey* (6 April 1998).

11. U.S. Conference of Mayors, *A Status Report on Hunger and Homelessness in America's Cities 1998* (December 1998), 1.

12. Lee Rainwater and Timothy M. Smeeding, "Doing Poorly: The Real Income of American Children in a Comparative Perspective," *Luxembourg Income Study*, Working Paper No. 127 (Syracuse, New York: Maxwell School of Citizenship and Public Affairs, Syracuse University, August 1995).

13. "Current Population Survey," U.S. Bureau of the Census, March 1998.

14. *One in Four: America's Youngest Poor*, National Center for Children in Poverty.

15. Larry Brown, "The Disease America's Never Cured," *Bread* (June 1997): 5.

16. Hunger Action Leadership Team, "I've Seen Hunger in My Community and It Looks Like This" (Tampa Bay, Fl., 1997).

Chapter 5: Focused Efforts

1. Terry R. Peel, "Stopping a War, Saving a Life: A Report From El Salvador," *America's Partnership with UNICEF* (New York: UNICEF/U.S. Committee for UNICEF, March 1997), 14.

2. UNICEF, *The State of the World's Children 1998* (Oxford: Oxford University Press), 97, extrapolated from child mortality rates cited in statistical table.

3. Ibid., 11, 65.

4. UNICEF, "Progress of Nations 1997" (New York), 15.

5. UNICEF, *The State of the World's Children 1986* (Oxford: Oxford University Press), 1.

6. Ibid., 10.

7. "Household Participation in the Food Stamps and WIC Programs Increases the Nutrient Intakes of Pre-School Children," *Journal of Nutrition* 128 (March 1998): 548–55.

8. B. Devaney and A. Schirin, "Infant Mortality Among Medicaid Newborns in Five States: The Effect of Prenatal Participation" (Princeton, N.J.: Mathematica Policy Research, 1993).

9. B. Devaney, L. Bilheimer and J. Shore, "The Savings in Medicaid Costs for Newborns and Their Mothers Resulting From Prenatal Participation in the WIC Program: Volume 2" (Princeton, N.J.: Mathematica Policy Research, 1991).

10. David Olds *et al.*, "Long-Term Effects of Nurse Home Visitation on Children's Criminal and Antisocial Behavior," *Journal of the American Medical Association* 280, no. 14 (1998): 1238–44.

Chapter 6: The Way Out

1. U.N. Development Program (UNDP), *Human Development Report 1998* (New York: Oxford University Press, 1998), 206.

2. Ibid.

3. Paul Brown, "Man's Greed Fuels Global Bonfire," *The Guardian* (17 December 1997).

4. Amartya Sen and Jean Dreze, *Hunger and Public Action* (Oxford: Clarendon, 1989).

5. Freedom House, *Freedom in the World: The Annual Survey of Political Rights and Civil Liberties 1997–1998* (New Brunswick: Transaction Publishers, 1998), 5.

6. World Bank, *1998 World Development Indicators* (Washington: World Bank, 1998), 104. Also the District of Columbia Public Health Commission, Division of Research and Statistics.

Chapter 7: You Can't Save Forests If People Are Starving

1. International Food Policy Research Institute (IFPRI). *Feeding the World, Preventing Poverty, and Protecting the Earth: A 2020 Vision* (Washington: IFPRI, 1996), 10.

Chapter 8: Too Many People?

1. U.N. Population Division (UNPD), *World Population Prospects: 1998 Revision*, forthcoming. The 1750–1940 data shown in the table are from www.undp.org/popin/wtrends/histor.html, accessed 29 October 1998.

2. Ibid.

3. Erla Zwingle, "Women and Population," *National Geographic*, October 1998, 39.

Chapter 9: Too Little Food?

1. Adapted from T. R. Reid, "Feeding the Planet," *National Geographic*, October 1998, 74.

2. Ibid., 58–59.

3. Gordon Conway, *The Doubly Green Revolution: Food for all in the 21st Century* (New York: Penguin Press, 1997), 41.

4. World Hunger Education Service, *Beachell and Khush: 30 Years of Rice Research*, available from http://www.brown.edu/Departments/World_Hunger_Program/hungerweb./HN/Articles/DEPTS/AGRICULT.html

5. Marc J. Cohen and Jashinta D'Costa, "Overview of Hunger," *What Governments Can Do: Hunger 1997*, ed. Marc J. Cohen (Silver Spring, Md.: Bread for the World Institute, 1996), 23.

6. BICO reports. http://www.fas.usda.gov/scriptsw/bico/bico_frm.idc

7. U.N. World Food Program, "1997 Food Aid Flows," *The Food Aid Monitor*, May 1998, 1.

8. Economic Research Service/U.S. Department of Agriculture, "Structural and Financial Characteristics of U.S. Farms, 1993," (Washington: ERS/USDA, 1993).

9. *FAO Production Yearbook*, vol. 47 (Rome: Food and Agriculture Organization of the United Nations, 1993), 3.

10. Gregg Easterbrook. "Forgotten Benefactor of Humanity." *The Atlantic* 279, no. 1 (January 1997): 81.

11. Ibid., 75.

12. Lester Brown and Hal Kane, *Full House* (New York: Norton, 1994), 60. See also Lester Brown, "Higher Crop Yields? Don't Bet the Farm on Them," *World Watch* (July/August 1997): 8–17.

13. Nikos Alexandratos, "The Outlook for World Food and Agriculture to Year 2010," *Population and Food in the Early 21st Century*, ed. Nurul Islam (Washington: International Food Policy Research Institute, 1995), 25–48.

14. Lester R. Brown, Gary Gardner and Brian Halweil, *Beyond Malthus: Sixteen Dimensions of the Population Program*, Worldwatch Paper #143 (Washington: Worldwatch Institute, September 1998), 16.

15. Ibid., 17.

16. See Lester R. Brown, *Who Will Feed China? A Wake-up Call for a Small Planet*, (New York: W. W. Norton, 1995).

17. Paul Simon, *Tapped Out: The Coming World Crisis in Water and What We Can Do About It* (New York: Welcome Rain, 1998), 85–124.

18. Ibid., 6.

19. Jane Sutton, "Mozambique: Peace and Promise," *World Vision* (August/September 1996): 20–21.

Chapter 10: Creating Good Jobs

1. Former executive director of Oxfam America.

2. Marc J. Cohen and Don Reeves, "Globalization, Governments and Politics," *Hunger in a Global Economy: Hunger 1998*, ed. Marc J. Cohen (Silver Spring, Md.: Bread for the World Institute, 1997), 25.

3. Ibid.

4. FINCA International, "Tibiwa's Story" (Washington: FINCA, 1998), in-house document.

Chapter 11: Investing in People

1. Statement while president of Second Harvest. Now prioress, Mount St. Benedict.

2. U.N. figures as reported by Suzanne Daley, "In Zambia, the Abandoned Generation," *The New York Times*, 18 September 1998.

3. U.N. Population Division, *World Population Prospects: 1998 Revision*, forthcoming, as reported by Youssef M. Ibrahim, "AIDS Is Slashing Africa's Population, U.N. Survey Finds," *The New York Times*, 28 October 1998.

4. Children's Defense Fund, *The State of America's Children* (Washington: Children's Defense Fund, 1998), 50.

5. Ernesto Pollit, foreword to *Statement on the Link Between Nutrition and Cognitive Development in Children* (Medford, MA: Center on Hunger, Poverty and Nutrition Policy, Tufts University School of Nutrition, 1995), 3.

6. Rachel Jones, "When You Have to Pretend You're Not Hungry," *The Washington Post*, 23 August 1996.

7. U.S. Department of Agriculture, Nutrition Program Facts, posted at www.usda.gov/fcs/stamps. Accessed 22 October 1998.

Chapter 12: Welfare Reform

1. Based on Alexandra Marks, "Less Welfare, Same Poverty in Heart of Appalachia," *The Christian Science Monitor*, 6 May 1988.

2. William Raspberry, "Poor—and Different from You and Me," *The Washington Post*, 17 November 1997.

3. Marc J. Cohen and Don Reeves, "The Raging Debate About U.S. Poverty," *What Governments Can Do: Hunger 1997*, ed. Marc J. Cohen (Silver Spring, Md.: Bread for the World Institute, 1996), 44.

4. Bread for the World Institute, *Let's Get Real About Welfare* (1994), 20.

5. Center on Hunger, Poverty and Nutrition Policy, Tufts University, "Are the States Improving the Lives of Poor Families?" (Medford, MA: Center on Hunger, Poverty and Nutrition Policy, Tufts University, February 1998), 1.

6. Bread for the World Institute, *TAHL Tales* (1998).

7. Lynette Engelhardt, "The Changing Politics of U.S. Welfare Policy," *The Changing Politics of Hunger: Hunger 1999*, ed. James Riker (Bread for the World Institute, 1998), 75.

Chapter 13: Women Bear the Brunt

1. Adapted from Nicholas D. Kristof, "As Asian Economies Shrink, Women Are Squeezed Out." *The New York Times*, 6 June 1998.

2. Hunger Action Leadership Team, "I've Seen Hunger in My Community and It Looks Like This" (Tampa Bay, Fl., 1997).

3. Cecelia A. Snyder, "Gender Discrimination." *Causes of Hunger: Hunger 1995*, ed. Marc J. Cohen (Bread for the World Institute, 1994), 87.

4. Ibid., 90

5. U.N. Fund for Population, *The State of World Population 1997*, ed. Alex Marshall, 18.

6. Sylvia Nasar, "Indian Wins Nobel Award in Economics," *The New York Times*, 15 October 1998.

7. Marc Cohen, "Update on Global Hunger," *Hunger in a Global Economy: Hunger 1998* (1997), 19 and 86.

8. Nicholas D. Kristof. "As Asian Economies Shrink, Women Are Squeezed Out." *The New York Times*, 6 June 1998.

9. U.S. Bureau of the Census, *Poverty in the United States: 1997* (September 1997).

10. U.S. Department of Agriculture, *Household Food Security in the United States* (September 1997), E-2.

11. Children's Defense Fund, *The State of America's Children: Yearbook 1998* (Washington: Children's Defense Fund, 1998), 13.

12. Evangelicals for Social Action (ESA) is doing a series of studies about how to reduce poverty. ESA is looking afresh at proposals that are usually associated with political conservatives as well as ideas associated with political liberals. Ron Sider will summarize the findings in a book to be published in 1999.

13. James D. Wolfensohn, president, the World Bank, "Women and the Transformation of the 21st Century," address to the Fourth U.N. Conference on Women, Beijing, 15 September 1995.
14. Ibid.

Chapter 14: Racism and Hunger

1. U.S. Census Bureau figures for 1997.
2. The Africa Fund, *South Africa Fact Sheet 1995* (New York).
3. U.N. Development Program, *Human Development Report 1994* (New York: Oxford University Press, 1994), 98.
4. U.S. Bureau of the Census, *Poverty in the United States: 1997* (September 1997), C2–C5.
5. U.S. Department of Agriculture, *Household Food Security in the United States in 1995*, (September 1997), E1.
6. Ibid.
7. Bureau of Labor Statistics, *Labor Force Statistics from the Current Population Survey*, found on http://146.142.4.24/cgi-bin/surveymost on 30 October 1998.
8. U.S. Bureau of the Census, "Money Income in the United States: 1997," *Current Population Reports* (Washington: U.S. Government Printing Office, 1998), 60–200.
9. Ibid., C6–C8.
10. Amartya Sen, *Mortality as an Indicator of Economic Success and Failure* (Florence, Italy: UNICEF, 1995), 22–25.

Chapter 15: Two Cheers for Capitalism

1. From *Woodstock Report*, No. 46, June 1996, excerpted in *What Governments Can Do: Hunger 1997*, ed. Marc J. Cohen (Bread for the World Institute, 1996), 38.

Chapter 16: The Global Economy

1. Don Reeves, "Trade, Poverty Reduction and Economic Opportunity," *Hunger in a Global Economy: Hunger 1998*, ed. Marc J. Cohen (Silver Spring, Md.: Bread for the World Institute, 1997), 32.
2. U.N. Development Program, *Human Development Report 1999* (New York: Oxford University Press, 1998), 30.
3. James Gustave Speth, "Non-Benign Neglect: America and the Developing World in the Era of Globalization," address, National Press Club (Washington: 14 October 1998), 2.
4. Marc J. Cohen, "World Hunger in a Global Economy," *Hunger in a Global Economy: Hunger 1998* (Bread for the World Institute, 1997), 13.
5. Marc J. Cohen and Don Reeves, "Globalization, Government, and Politics," *Hunger in a Global Economy: Hunger 1998*, 29.

Chapter 17: Does Trade Hurt or Help?

1. Martin Ravallion and Shaohua Chen, "What Can New Survey Data Tell Us About Recent Changes in Distribution and Poverty?" *World Bank Economic Review*, May 1997.
2. World Bank, *World Development Indicators 1998* (Washington: World Bank, 1998).
3. Renee Marlin-Bennett, "Agricultural Trade and Food Security," *Hunger in a Global Economy: Hunger 1998*, ed. Marc J. Cohen (Silver Spring, Md.: Bread for the World Institute. 1997), 48.
4. Ethan B. Kapstein, Humphrey Institute, University of Minnesota, personal communication to David Beckmann, 31 January 1999.

5. U.N. Research Institute for Social Development, *Structural Adjustment, Global Integration and Social Democracy* (Geneva, Switzerland, 1998), 2.

6. Michelle Tooley, "Economic Justice and People of Faith" (report of the Witness for Peace Delegation to Nicaragua and Washington D.C., 9–24 July 1996).

7. International Labor Organization, *Child Labor: Targeting the Intolerable* (Geneva: ILO, 1996), 3.

8. Renee Marlin-Bennett, op. cit., 49–50.

Chapter 18: International Investment and Debt

1. A public letter, October 1998.

2. "Private Capital Flows Up Despite Asia Crisis, Aid Flows Dwindle," *World Bank News*, 2 April 1998, 1–2.

3. World Bank, *Private Capital Flows to Developing Countries* (Washington: World Bank, 1997), 7.

4. United Nations, *World Investment Report 1997* (New York: United Nations, 1997), Annex 229–30.

5. Nicholas D. Kristof, "The Human Crisis: Asian Crisis Deals Setbacks to Women." *The New York Times*, 11 June 1998.

6. World Bank, *Global Development Finance 1998* (Washington: World Bank, 1998), 150 and 184.

7. UNICEF, *The State of the World's Children 1997* (New York: Oxford University Press, 1997), 53.

8. A. W. Clausen, "Third World Debt and Global Recovery," *The Development Challenge of the Eighties* (Washington: The World Bank, 1986).

Chapter 19: Crumbs from the Table

1. Address to the Protestant Council of the City of New York, 8 November 1963.

2. Program on International Policy Attitudes, *Americans and Foreign Aid: A Study of American Public Attitudes* (College Park, Md.: University of Maryland, 1995).

3. *At the Crossroads* (Silver Spring, Md.: Bread for the World Institute, 1995), 35–36.

4. "Kampala Summit Calls for New Partnerships in Africa," *World Bank News*, 5 February 1998, 2.

5. "Economic and Development Indicators," *Hunger in a Global Economy: Hunger 1998*, ed. Marc J. Cohen (Silver Spring, Md.: Bread for the World Institute, 1997), 102.

Chapter 20: The World Bank and the IMF

1. "For Want of Feed, Indonesia Is Losing Its Chickens."

2. *World Bank Annual Report 1998* (Washington: The World Bank), xii.

3. Witness for Peace, "A High Price to Pay: Structural Adjustment in Nicaragua" (1996), 8–10.

4. Kathleen A. Selvaggio and Marc J. Cohen, "Poor Country Debt: Payable in Hunger," *Hunger in a Global Economy: Hunger 1998*, ed. Marc J. Cohen (Silver Spring, Md.: Bread for the World Institute, 1997), 77.

Chapter 21: Charity Is Not Enough

1. *Second Harvest 1997 Annual Report*, 10.

2. This includes both government and private contributions. For example, of the $2.1 billion that Catholic Charities USA and its network of 1,400 local agencies received in

1996, $1.3 billion came from the government and $335 million from private contributions. Most of the rest came from service fees.

3. *Second Harvest 1997 Annual Report*, 10.

4. Tufts University Center on Hunger, Poverty, and Nutrition Policy and Second Harvest.

5. The national nutrition programs cost $39 billion in 1998.

6. Lt. Colonel Paul E. Bollwahn, The Salvation Army National Headquarters, personal communication to David Beckmann, 29 January 1999.

7. Janet Poppendieck, *Sweet Charity? Emergency Food and the End of Entitlement* (New York: Viking Penguin, 1998), 221–22.

8. Ibid., 301–03.

9. Richard A. Hoehn, "Feeding People—Half of Overcoming Hunger," *Transforming the Politics of Hunger: Hunger 1994*, ed. Marc J. Cohen (Silver Spring, Md.: Bread for the World Institute, 1993), 17.

10. James H. Michael, *Development Cooperation: Efforts and Policies of the Members of the Development Assistance Committee, 1997 Report* (Paris: Organization for Economic Cooperation and Development, 1998), A20.

Chapter 22: The Government Has to Do Its Part

1. Quoted by Ronald J. Sider and Fred Clark, "Should We Give Up on Government?" *Christianity Today*, 2 March 1998, 53.

2. Reinhold Niebuhr, *Moral Man and Immoral Society* (New York: Charles Scribner's Sons, 1932), 127.

3. Ronald J. Sider and Fred Clark, op. cit., 54.

4. K. Porter, W. Primus, L. Rawlings and E. Rosenbaum, "Strengths of the Safety Net: How the EITC, Social Security and Other Current Programs Affect Poverty" (Washington: Center on Budget and Policy Priorities, March 1998).

5. *The Washington Post*/Henry J. Kaiser Family Foundation/Harvard University entitlement poll, March 13–23, 1997.

Chapter 23: Guns and Bread

1. James C. McKinley Jr., "Fueled by Drought and War, Starvation Returns to Sudan," *The New York Times*, 24 July 1998.

2. Dwight D. Eisenhower, "The Chance for Peace," address to the American Society of Newspaper Editors, 16 April 1953.

3. U.N. High Commissioner for Refugees, information posted at www.unhcr.ch, accessed 30 January 1999.

4. UNICEF, *The State of the World's Children, 1996* (Oxford: Oxford University Press, 1996), 21.

5. U.N. Development Program, *Human Development Report 1996* (New York: UNDP/Oxford University Press, 1996), 24

6. UNICEF, op. cit., 26.

7. "Bringing Life Back to Angola's Countryside," *World Bank News*, 23 April 1998.

8. Tim Zimmerman, "Why Do Countries Fall Apart?" *U.S. News & World Report*, 12 February 1996.

9. U.N. Development Program, *Human Development Report: 1997* (UNDP, 1997), 215.

10. Laura Tyson, "Leadership in a Crisis," *The Washington Post*, 22 January 1998.

11. Lawrence J. Korb, "Exaggerated Expenses," *The Washington Post*, 14 May 1998.

Chapter 24: Democracy and Human Rights

1. "In One Poor African Nation, Democracy Thrives."

2. "Nigeria, in Free Fall, Seethes Under General," *The New York Times*, 4 April 1998.

3. Keith B. Richburg, "Beyond a Wall of Secrecy, Devastation," *The Washington Post*, 19 October 1997.

Chapter 25: Can We Afford to End Hunger?

1. Bread for the World Institute, *At the Crossroads: The Future of Foreign Aid* (1995), 30.

2. Ralph H. Henderson, "Immunizations: Going the Extra Mile," *The Progress of Nations 1998* (New York: UNICEF), 13.

3. U.N. Development Program (UNDP), *Human Development Report 1998* (New York: Oxford University Press, 1998), 37.

4. J. Dirck Stryker and Jeffrey C. Metzel, "Meeting the Food Summit Target and the United States Contribution," APAP III Research Report 1038, Prepared for the U.S. Agency for International Development.

5. UNDP, op. cit., 37.

6. Food Research and Action Center (Washington) and Center on Hunger, Poverty and Nutrition Policy (Tufts University), unpublished memo, 1992.

7. Scheduled for November 1999 publication.

Chapter 26: Transforming the Politics of Hunger

1. Quoted by James A. Cogswell, "Crisis of Confidence in U.S. Aid to Poor Nations," *The Causes of Hunger*, ed. William Byron (New York: Paulist Press, 1982), 159.

2. Opinion Research Corporation, Princeton, New Jersey, "Pre-Wave Omnibus Research," 1997, unpublished; Leo Shapiro and Associates, Chicago, Illinois, "Second Harvest Tracking Survey of the Public, 1995," unpublished.

3. Steven Kull, I. M. Destler and Clay Ramsey, *The Foreign Policy Gap: How Policymakers Misread the Public* (College Park, Md.: Center for International and Security Studies at the University of Maryland, 1997).

4. Robert Wuthnow, Virginia A. Hodkinson and Associates, *Exploring the Role of Religion in America's Voluntary Sector* (San Francisco: Jossey-Bass Inc., 1990), 112.

5. Kraig Klaudt, "Transforming Media Coverage of Hunger," *Transforming the Politics of Hunger: Hunger 1994*, ed. Marc J. Cohen (Silver Spring, Md.: Bread for the World Institute, 1993), 74.

Chapter 28: You Can Make a Difference!

1. Attributed to Edmund Burke, *Bartlett's Familiar Quotations* (Boston: Little, Brown & Co., 1992), 332.

2. Based on the amount raised by the 34 successful candidates for the U.S. Senate in 1998, as reported by Common Cause.

3. *Insight* 21 October 1996, 32.

4. Study financed by the Joyce Foundation of Chicago, cited by Bob Herbert, "The Donor Class," *The New York Times on the Web* (19 July 1998).

5. Leon Howell, "The Politics of Hunger in the United States," *The Changing Politics of Hunger: Hunger 1999*, ed. James Riker (Silver Spring, Md.: Bread for the World Institute, 1998), 65.

Acknowledgments

We are indebted to more people in more ways than can be adequately acknowledged. Michael Rubinstein, Andrea Jeyaveeran, Margaret Cohen Lipton, Derek Miller and Lynora Williams helped with the writing. Dolly Youssef managed the process of preparing the manuscript. Other Bread for the World staff Mai Bull, Jashinta D'Costa, Lynette Engelhardt Stott, Sara Grusky, Richard Hoehn, Barbara Howell, Elena McCollim, Nathan Raybeck, Jim Riker and Don Williams also made important contributions.

Pat Ayres, Pat Burge, John Carr, Peter Carry, Marc Cohen, Gary Cook, Walter Grazer, Janet Green, John Halvorson, Rebekah Jordan, Ken Lutgen, Ellis Malone, Ron Sider, Joel Underwood, Betty Voskuil and Jim Wallis read all or parts of the manuscript and offered valuable suggestions. Many Bread for the World members suggested questions that are addressed in the book.

The second chapter draws material from a previous book by Arthur Simon, *Christian Faith and Public Policy: No Grounds for Divorce* (Grand Rapids: William B. Eerdmans, 1987, 15–29), that is used with permission.

We are grateful to Don Brophy, Donna Crilly, Andrew LePeau and their colleagues at Paulist Press and InterVarsity Press for editing, producing and marketing the book. We especially appreciate the collaboration between these two fine publishers in making this book available to a wide array of U.S. Christians.

None of those who helped with the book deserve blame for its shortcomings. All have our gratitude.

Janet Beckmann and Rosamund Simon, our wives, deserve special credit for patience and understanding, along with the extra load they and our children, Andrew and John Beckmann and Leah Simon, willingly took on while the book was being written.

Most of all, we thank those to whom this book is dedicated: Bread for the World members across the country, whose commitment and energy contribute greatly toward ending hunger in God's world.

About the Authors

David Beckmann has been president of Bread for the World since 1991. Beckmann is a Lutheran minister and an economist. He holds earned degrees from Yale, Christ Seminary and the London School of Economics and honorary doctorates from Capitol University and the Berkeley Divinity School at Yale.

At his ordination, he was called to be a "missionary-economist." He served in a church-supported development program in rural Bangladesh. He then moved to the World Bank, where he worked on slum improvement projects, later wrote speeches for the president of the Bank and finally led the World Bank's efforts to engage with religious, environmental and other grass-roots groups around the world.

Under Beckmann's leadership, Bread for the World has grown in influence and has been systematically working to build the broader movement to overcome hunger and poverty.

Beckmann's books include *Friday Morning Reflections at the World Bank* and, together with Richard Hoehn, *Transforming the Politics of Hunger*.

He is married and has two children.

Art Simon founded Bread for the World in 1974. As pastor of a Lutheran church on the Lower East Side of New York City, he was struck by the magnitude of hunger and poverty in his community and around the world. So in 1972, he gathered a small group of Catholics and Protestants who decided to launch a citizens' movement against hunger.

Simon built Bread for the World into an effective movement of 44 thousand members. Since retiring, he directed the Washington office of the Christian Children's Fund for a few years and has been active in seeking endowments for Bread for the World and Bread for the World Institute. In 1991 he received a presidential award for lifetime achievement against hunger.

He has written a number of books including *Bread for the World* and, with his brother Paul, *The Politics of World Hunger*.

He is married and the father of three sons and a daughter.